T0008491

'Learned and wise, this is a book that [illegible] Christians may find a startling feat: a demonstration that orthodoxy is far more radical and interesting a concept than heresy.'
Tom Holland, author of *Dominion: The Making of the Western Mind*

'A timely and highly relevant work. Dr Tomlin offers a powerful defence of Christian orthodoxy, and opens up its expansive, generous and life-giving vision.'
Alister McGrath, Andreas Idreos Professor of Science and Religion, University of Oxford

'The word "orthodoxy" scares us. It smells of authoritarianism and oppression. But it should not. Properly understood, it can both protect and liberate. That is the message of Graham Tomlin's masterly *Navigating a World of Grace*, in which, with his characteristic erudition and wisdom, he rescues "orthodoxy" from the darkness and shows how it reflects, for all of us, a great light.'
Nick Spencer, Senior Fellow, Theos

'With typical clarity and depth, Graham Tomlin shows that the life offered to us in the great Christian creeds is a life enabled by the reality of the sheer grace of God. We navigate the rivers of mercy, aided by these profound insights into the nature and purpose of God.'
Jane Williams, McDonald Professor in Christian Theology, St Mellitus College

The Rt Revd Dr Graham Tomlin is Bishop of Kensington and President of St Mellitus College. He served as Chaplain of Jesus College Oxford and Vice Principal of Wycliffe Hall, Oxford, where he taught within the Theology Faculty of the University on Historical Theology. He was the first Dean of St Mellitus College. He is the editor (with Nathan Eddy) of *The Bond of Peace* and the author of many books and articles, including *The Power of the Cross: Theology and the Death of Christ in Paul, Luther and Pascal*, *Looking Through the Cross* (the Archbishop of Canterbury's Lent Book for 2014), *The Widening Circle: Priesthood as God's Way of Blessing the World* and *Luther's Gospel: Reimagining the World*.

NAVIGATING A WORLD OF GRACE

The promise of generous orthodoxy

Graham Tomlin

First published in Great Britain in 2022

Society for Promoting Christian Knowledge
36 Causton Street
London SW1P 4ST
www.spck.org.uk

British Library Cataloguing-in-Publication Data
A catalogue record for this book is available from the British Library

ISBN 978–0–281–08285–8
eBook ISBN 978–0–281–08286–5

1 3 5 7 9 10 8 6 4 2

Typeset by Fakenham Prepress Solutions, Fakenham, Norfolk NR21 8NL
Printed in Great Britain by Clays Ltd, Elcograf S.p.A.

eBook by Fakenham Prepress Solutions, Fakenham, Norfolk NR21 8NL

Produced on paper from sustainable sources

'The more I considered Christianity, the more I found that while it had established a rule and order, the chief aim of that order was to give room for good things to run wild.'
G. K. Chesterton

'We make the first and greatest of our mistakes in religion when we begin with ourselves, our petty feelings and needs, ideas and capacities. The Creed sweeps us up past all this to God, the objective Fact, and His mysterious self-giving to us.'
Evelyn Underhill

In grateful memory of
Ivor Tomlin (1922–1991) and Anne Tomlin (1924–2020)

Contents

Contents

Introduction

When I was growing up, my family spent most of our summer holidays in the west of Ireland. I would while away hours fishing in rock pools, playing on the beach, eating ice cream and swimming in the (usually freezing) Atlantic in the days before wetsuits. The coast of County Clare is a wild and rugged place. This really is the harsh western edge of Europe with nothing between the sea cliffs and the eastern seaboard of the USA 4,000 miles away. It's not without reason that the early Celtic monks built some of their spectacular settlements on remote islands just off this coast, such as the Blaskets (the very name conjures up bleak, howling sea winds) and Skellig Michael further south off the coast of Kerry.

We stayed in a small holiday town clustered around a gentle sandy beach. However, not far away on either side of that beach the land rose to great sea cliffs. At its highest, the Clare coast reaches up to the famous cliffs of Moher, 700 feet above the roaring waves below. On a wild, stormy day, this coastline can be a fearsome and exhilarating place.

There was one particular spot that always fascinated me: a large sea stack about half a mile off the coast with sheer cliffs, 200 feet high, on all sides. The stack was effectively an island, totally inaccessible to anyone but an experienced rock climber capable of swimming across treacherous seas and then scaling vertical cliffs of that size. It was called Bishop's Island because the remains of a sixth-century monastic settlement stood on the flat top of the stack, presumably peopled by fierce, hardy, rock-climbing monks. I would often gaze across in terror and fascination, imagining what it would be like to live in such a place.[1]

What drew me was the mixture of beauty, security and danger. The surface of the island was completely flat and on warm days you could picture yourself lying back, sunbathing, enjoying the spectacular views and feeling perfectly safe. I could even imagine myself playing games on the grassy surface, exploring the ancient ruins and spotting the sea birds landing on its gentle turf. And yet not far away were those ever-present sheer cliffs on all sides, threatening doom and destruction.

Imagine another island. This one doesn't have a name. It's where Robinson Crusoe landed after his shipwreck in Daniel Defoe's celebrated novel of 1719. Having run away from home, Crusoe has various adventures on the high seas, culminating in his ship foundering on rocks close to a small island off the coast of Venezuela. He finds himself washed up on an unhospitable, uninhabited strip of land, and his initial thoughts are that this is a grim, desolate place. His journal begins:

> September 30, 1659. I, poor miserable Robinson Crusoe, being shipwrecked, during a dreadful storm . . . came on shore on this dismal unfortunate island, which I called the Island of Despair, all the rest of the ship's company being drowned, and myself almost dead.[2]

After establishing a rather simple settlement, he begins to explore the rest of the island:

> Having now secured my habitation, as I thought, fully to my mind, I had a great desire to make a more perfect discovery of the island, and to see what other productions I might find, which I yet knew nothing of.[3]

As he does so, he makes a pleasing discovery:

> I found that side of the island where I now was much pleasanter than mine, the open or Savannah fields sweet, adorned with flowers and grass, and full of very fine woods. I saw abundance of parrots, and fain I would have caught one, if possible, to have kept it to be tame and taught it to speak to me.[4]

It turns out that the island is, in fact, much bigger than Crusoe had originally thought, with valleys, hills and a great variety of wild-life. He kills some animals for food and tames others as pets. This place of plenty and beauty offers him everything he needs for life and comfort apart, that is, from human company, which eventually arrives with 'man Friday' and a few other shipwrecked sailors towards the end of the book.

Keeping these two islands in mind, picture one more. Little Sark is a small piece of land that rises out of the English Channel not far from Guernsey. If you were to alight on Little Sark's south coast and begin to explore its fields and gentle sea cliffs, you'd be forgiven for thinking that this was an enclosed island in the middle of the sea. At its northern edge however, you would find that it is joined by an isthmus to the prosperous island of Sark itself, although the connecting ridge is so rocky that people would frequently be swept to their deaths from its crest before the current pathway was established. So, what seems like an island is, in fact, something a little different: though surrounded by sea, its north-west corner has a narrow route to a very much grander place.

Mapping the island of life

Imagine a combination of these three islands. Imagine landing on an island (possibly by helicopter!) that feels safe and secure, with rich soil, a comfortable flat area for building a house on and growing food, yet which is surrounded by fearsome cliffs that lead to destruction. Then imagine that this island is, in fact, a lot bigger than it immediately appears. It supports all kinds of extraordinary life and provides you with everything you need to live and to flourish yet, unlike Robinson Crusoe's island, it has other people and animals providing social as well as physical existence. But then imagine that the island is not actually a complete island at all, but that there is a way off it over a small narrow isthmus that leads to a much bigger and even more stunningly beautiful place beyond.

With this multifaceted picture in mind, consider the life into which we are born. We are pitched into a world we might imagine as a land that provides us with everything we need (even if it might not always be shared out fairly). We are invited to explore this place in all its variety and richness. However, although it offers many delights, we discover we need to explore with a degree of caution for there are cliffs all around and not every pathway leads somewhere healthy and good.

We then also realize that, even though the place feels like an island there is, in fact, a way off it: a narrow isthmus called death, which in Christian understanding is the pathway to something much greater and grander than we have ever known in this life.

To explore the island, it helps to have a map. An ideal map for such an island would outline all the interesting places to go and the different pathways that lead you to different sites, settlements and viewpoints. It would guide you through the complexity and variety of the island, helping you find your way. Yet it would also indicate the pathways that could lead you into danger by taking you near the cliffs at the edge of the island.

In this book, I would like to suggest that Christian orthodoxy offers us a map to the island of life. Far from being a narrow, restrictive set of beliefs, orthodoxy is liberating and creative. Through the Catholic creeds, it indicates what is important, what to see and what to investigate. It shows us the contours, the hills and the valleys, and helps us understand what is true about this land. Yet orthodoxy also has its shadow side: the concept of heresy. Heresies, in this image, are pathways, ways of thinking and believing, that may seem initially attractive but, if followed too far, will lead us towards the cliffs and eventually to destruction. In short, orthodoxy reveals a bigger world than we could ever imagine, while implicitly warning us about what could lead us in harmful directions.

G. K. Chesterton, the larger-than-life literary critic, writer and lay theologian, offers a similar idea in his book, *Orthodoxy*, of a space surrounded by danger:

We might fancy some children playing on the flat grassy top of some tall island in the sea. So long as there was a wall round the cliff's edge, they could fling themselves into every frantic game and make the place the noisiest of nurseries. But the walls were knocked down, leaving the naked peril of the precipice. They did not fall over; but when their friends returned to them, they were all huddled in terror in the centre of the island; and their song had ceased.[5]

Orthodoxy is a map that tells us where we can play and that makes sure that we don't go anywhere near the gaps in the wall around the island. It enables us to continue singing, safe from danger, until the time comes when we leave the island across the narrow ridge of death to a place that is even more expansive and wonderful than this. It helps us navigate a world of grace – a bigger and better world than we can imagine or deserve.

A generous orthodoxy

When I was involved in establishing St Mellitus College in 2007, we tried to bring together the mainstream traditions of the Church into a place where each could be valued within a broader framework of confident Christian faith, taking theology seriously and always expectant of the presence and work of the Holy Spirit among us.

The college's founders hit on the phrase 'generous orthodoxy' to describe what we were trying to do. A number of years on from there, and now working as a bishop in the Church of England with its many different traditions of faith, worship and prayer within the one Church, it seemed worthwhile to spend some time exploring in more detail what this generous orthodoxy might look like. The MacDonald Agape Foundation generously provided a grant to sponsor a research project into the meaning of the phrase. A series of conversations were held among St Mellitus staff, and a lecture series bringing theologians from around the world to reflect upon the idea was arranged. The results of those conversations and lectures were published in *The Bond of Peace: Exploring Generous Orthodoxy* (London, SPCK, 2021). That volume is a companion to this one, which is my own more personal take on the topic, and at several points during these chapters I will refer back to those very illuminating essays to help fill in our understanding of this idea.

The notion of generous orthodoxy originally came from the American theologian Hans Frei, who wrote:

> My own vision of what might be propitious for our day, split as we are, not so much into denominations as in two schools of thought, is that we need a kind of generous orthodoxy which would have in it an element of liberalism, and an element of evangelicalism.[6]

Frei imagined a form of Christian faith that transcended the various traditions of the Church, yet, at the same time, was deeply rooted in *the* tradition of the Church. It would return to a close, literal reading of Scripture while avoiding simplistic literal readings. He claimed that the literal sense of Scripture is the Christological sense, in that it centres around the resurrected Jesus, the figure whose presence the text offers us. He suggested that either the Christian faith gives a properly basic framework for interpreting the rest of reality, founded on the resurrection, which by definition can't be founded on anything deeper than itself, or it is not worth bothering about.

This book examines what a theology that took the best from different traditions of the Church might look like. It also tries to take orthodoxy, the 'language of the church', with real seriousness. Furthermore, it builds on Frei's insight that Christian faith, built on the resurrection, is either the foundation for a whole new way of understanding and living in the world or else it is nothing. While it borrows terms and concepts from other worldviews, it can't ultimately appeal to other sources or resources to establish its truth. Christian orthodoxy isn't an object in someone else's map of life, but instead it offers its own map for the invigorating journey of life, which is sorely needed in our own confusing times.

So often, the attempt has been made to fit the Christian gospel into the framework of other visions of the world, whether scientific rationalism, expressive individualism, political nationalism or whatever. Yet Christian orthodoxy is too big to fit within any other vision of the world because those visions are too small. As Robert Jenson puts it in relation to the neo-Darwinian story:

> The tale told by Scripture is too comprehensive to find place within so drastically curtailed a version of the facts. Indeed, the gospel story cannot fit within *any* other would-be metan-arrative because it is itself the only true metanarrative – or it is altogether false.[7]

In speaking of generous orthodoxy, I have often found people quite attracted to the 'generous' side of the phrase, but a little nervous about the 'orthodoxy'. The suspicion is that you can be 'generous' or 'orthodox' but not both. Orthodoxy has often gained the reputation, perhaps with some justification, of being a harsh and restrictive form of faith, and so people quite like the qualifying adjective 'generous' as it seems to soften a rather hard-edged moral and dogmatic outlook. In this book, I want to challenge the idea that 'generosity' and 'orthodoxy' are somehow opposed to, or even in tension with, one another. I want to show how orthodoxy is in its very nature generous in many senses of that word, but also how orthodoxy is all about forming people in generosity and is there-fore the right and appropriate way in which orthodoxy is to be held and celebrated.

As I write this book, I'm conscious of the debt I owe to many friends and colleagues at St Mellitus College over the years, of whom there are far too many to mention ('never start a list of people to thank' is a good piece of advice). I'm grateful for all the conversations, prayers, worship and exploration shared with fellow lecturers, students and others over that time as we navigated the reality and experience of building a generous orthodoxy together. I'm also aware of all that I have learned from colleagues, friends and clergy in the Diocese of London and particularly the Kensington Area since I became Bishop in 2015. We have a rich variety of forms of Christian life, prayer and spirituality in our Area. I have been enriched by each one and am grateful for my fellow workers in this part of the Christian vineyard.

I'm also grateful to all at SPCK who helped the book come to light, especially Alison Barr, and to several friends who have helped shape the book through their conversation, reading of the text and comments on it, including Jane Williams, Simon Cuff, Graham Charkham, Steve Hellyer, David Emerton, Hannah Steele and Alex Irving. I'm also grateful to Ron and Celia Morgan in whose delightful home in Pembrokeshire some of the book was written. Much of it was written on a period of study leave from my post as the Bishop of Kensington and I am grateful to Bishop Ric Thorpe, the Archdeacon of Middlesex, Richard Frank and Emma Hughes in particular, who held the reins while I was away. As always, I'm profoundly grateful to God for my family, to Sam, Sian, Josh and Jenni with whom I have shared many rich theological conversations, and particularly to Janet, my wife, greatest friend and wisest counsellor.

Peter MacDonald of the MacDonald Agape Foundation has become a good friend and I'm grateful to him and the trustees for the funding that enabled the research project to take place. It has been a fascinating and enriching process and my hope and prayer is that this book will expand our horizons and deepen our gratitude for what those great Christians of the past have bequeathed to us in the great gift of the generosity of Christian orthodoxy.

Part 1

THE GENEROSITY
OF ORTHODOXY

1

The origins of orthodoxy

The word 'orthodoxy' generates very different reactions. For some people, it conveys the idea of something rigid, inflexible and even oppressive. In the name of orthodoxy and to ensure conformity to it, inquisitions were set up and fires lit to burn heretics. A desire to ensure strict adherence to orthodox thinking has, in the past, often been used as a means of oppression and control.

To others, it means a restrictive limit to independent thought. Too fixed an orthodoxy prevents the kind of free thinking that is essential to a creative and resourceful society. The Victorian philosopher John Stuart Mill believed that any healthy society needed to allow for a freedom of thought that could break beyond the bounds of orthodoxy. In fact, it is precisely freedom of thought, not a fixed, indisputable orthodoxy, that is the condition for human progress. Mill wrote of how orthodoxy and the fear of heresy 'cramped the mental development' of timid minds, who needed to be liberated to think freely.[1]

For others, orthodoxy indicates something a little dull, dutiful and predictable. It conjures ideas of a list of 'orthodox' beliefs that have to be agreed or assented to if a person is to qualify as a Christian of whatever kind.

One of the ways Christianity is different from other religions is that it is the only one of the major world faiths that has a sense of doctrinal orthodoxy expressed in creeds.[2] Buddhism, Hinduism, and even other monotheistic religions such as Judaism and Islam have particular prayers, elaborate scriptures or simple statements of belief, but nothing that corresponds to what Christians have in the carefully worded and long-pondered creeds of the Church.

Creeds, or simple statements of belief, have their origins in the earliest instincts of the Christian faith. Jesus himself quotes the nearest thing the Jewish faith has to a creed, the Shema: 'Hear, O Israel: the Lord our God, the Lord is one' (Mark 12.29 quoting from Deut. 6.4). In the New Testament, we find several texts that may have served as credal formulae in the earliest churches, such as the famous hymn to Christ in Philippians 2, or this one:

> He was revealed in flesh,
> vindicated in spirit,
> seen by angels,
> proclaimed among Gentiles,
> believed in throughout the world,
> taken up in glory.
> (1 Tim. 3.16)

From early days, Christians found ways to formulate their faith into these pithy, short summaries. The question is, why did they feel the need to do this while other religions have felt little need to do so?

The contexts of early Christianity

Creeds were born in the context of oppression. From its earliest days, Christianity arose not as a faith of the powerful but on the margins. Although it moved into the centres of power in Rome and Byzantium in the fourth century, Christians lived under the shadow of the disapproval or suspicion of neighbours and authorities before that time. This was rarely outright violent persecution, but it was a fairly continuous note of dislike and suspicion from pagan neighbours, which from time to time broke out into local hostility.

It is worth remembering that most of the signatories of the original Nicene Creed, the 250 or so bishops present at the Council of 325 AD, had emerged from the fires of persecution themselves. We shouldn't imagine a group of powerful, privileged bureaucrats opining on abstract and irrelevant doctrine, but people who had lost friends, members of their churches, and who bore in their bodies the scars of beatings and in their minds the memory of harsh imprisonment in the Diocletian persecution that lingered in recent memory. Some had spent years in exile or working in salt mines for this faith they were called to define and defend at Nicaea. The Church became a powerful global institution in the Middle Ages, but in the fourth century, despite the new imperial patronage, this was a group of scarred, oppressed people wanting to guard something so precious that they would have given their lives for it if they had been asked to. It must have been bizarre for them to meet in the presence of the emperor and his bodyguard, only 20 years or so since his predecessor was dedicated to the elimination of the Church.

This background of oppression also helps explain the need for creeds. As the early Church baptized new converts, they needed a way to ensure the faith of these applicants was genuine, to make sure they knew what they were getting themselves into, to check that motives were as pure as they could be and to test that those joining the church were to be trusted. Early Christian texts reflect this blend of eagerness, yet cautiousness about welcoming in enquirers. We find this in New Testament writings such as 2 and 3 John. It also appears in *The Didache* (a manual for Christian life and teaching usually dated around 70 AD) with its cautious words about welcoming those who 'come in the name of the Lord', yet reminding the church of the need to test them carefully,[3] and Hippolytus' *On the Apostolic Tradition* from Rome in the mid-third century, with its list of detailed questions to be asked of anyone wanting to join the church.[4]

From the second through to the third century and beyond, preparation for baptism consisted of potential candidates entering the catechumenate, a long process of preparation for initiation into the faith, which would often involve teaching from the local bishop on the content of that faith.[5] It would involve the handing over (*traditio*) of the faith to the potential Christian, for them to learn a summary of Christian belief by heart, and the subsequent *redditio* (handing back) of that faith through recitation as part of preparation for baptism.

When it came to the actual baptism itself, from an early time, it seems candidates would be asked questions so they could publicly confess the faith they were being baptized into. *On the Apostolic Tradition* depicts baptismal candidates being asked three questions:

- Do you believe in God the Father Almighty?
- Do you believe in Christ Jesus, the Son of God, who was born of the Holy Spirit and Mary the Virgin, who was crucified under Pontius Pilate and was dead, and rose on the third day alive from the dead, and ascended in the heavens, and sits at the right hand of the Father, and will come to judge the living and the dead?
- Do you believe in the Holy Spirit and the holy church and the resurrection of the flesh?[6]

Each time, the candidate was supposed to answer simply 'I believe'.[7]

We can see in these questions the beginnings of creeds with their threefold formula of belief in Father, Son and Holy Spirit. A small, despised minority needs to guard its boundaries and protect its identity. Short statements of core belief to test newcomers were one way to do exactly that.

Second, creeds arose from the urgent need to recommend and explain Christian faith to a pagan world. Second-century apologists such as Aristides, Justin Martyr, Athenagoras and, beyond them, theologians such as Origen in his work *Contra Celsum* written in the mid-third century, all wrote specifically to commend and defend emerging Christian belief from its detractors, both Jewish and pagan. These were often connected closely to the previous point about persecution. So, for example, Justin Martyr's Second Apology, one of the earliest pieces of Christian apologetics we have, was occasioned by a recent incident in Rome where a Christian woman had sought a divorce from her abusive pagan husband, who in turn had accused her Christian teacher, Ptolomaeus, who was then hauled before the authorities and punished purely on the charge of being a Christian. Persecution of Christians gave an urgency to the need to defend and commend Christian faith publicly.

In the course of these writings, a common core of Christian faith began to emerge as defining the points where it cut across Jewish and pagan beliefs such as the idea that God became incarnate in Jesus Christ (despite Jewish monotheism and Platonic suspicion of physical matter) or the resurrection of Jesus (despite Jewish postponement of resurrection to the future, and pagan disbelief in any idea of a renewal of the body in a future life). Orthodoxy emerged as a by-product of the impulse to share this faith, to show how it did a better job of enabling people to live and die well than the various pagan cults or philosophical systems on offer at the time.

The third aspect of the historical context that helps explain the rise of credal orthodoxy was the series of debates that developed on the fringes of the early Christian community around the question of the nature of Christian belief. Questions arose in Christian communities such as: what would be the role of the Hebrew Scriptures in the new movement, and what should they think of teachers like Marcion, who argued that the churches didn't need to read them because they referred to a different God? Or what should the Church make of the ideas coming from what became known as Gnostic groups and teachers? And who, out of the various teachers and leaders in the earliest churches, represented true Christian faith in a particular place?

At the forefront of the response were figures such as Irenaeus of Lyons, Tertullian and Origen. In his writings, Irenaeus refers to a 'rule of faith'. This seems to have been a loose summary of Christian faith, coming in different forms with which they were all familiar and which was regarded as a summary of the teaching of the apostles.[8] Irenaeus could also be said to have invented the category of heresy in his classic work *Against Heresies*, written around 180 AD. After giving a summary of the convoluted ideas of the various Gnostic teachers, he gives a brief summary of Christian belief by way of contrast and then adds:

The Church, having received this preaching and this faith, although scattered throughout the whole world, yet, as if occupying but one house, carefully preserves it. She also believes these points [of doctrine] just as if she had but one soul, and one and the same heart, and she proclaims them, and teaches them, and hands them down, with perfect harmony, as if she possessed only one mouth. For, although the languages of the world are dissimilar, yet the import of the tradition is one and the same.[9]

Orthodoxy here arises out of the need for unity, identity and definition. If Gnosticism, with its elaborate Neoplatonic plethora of divine and semi-divine beings, its hostility to the idea of creation and its view of a disembodied salvation was inadequate, these early Christian thinkers needed some marker that defined Christian belief and identity over against systems of thought and life that were similar enough to cause controversy, yet different enough to threaten Christian identity. In particular, with the Gnostic separation of the doctrine of creation from that of redemption, the God of the Old Testament from the God of the New, creeds were an assertion of the essential unity of the Bible, what Christopher Seitz describes as 'letting Scripture come to its natural, two-testament expression'.[10]

Irenaeus is also conscious of the global nature of this new faith. It had local roots in towns and settlements across the empire, but these communities needed a common identity, and a common statement of the animating beliefs that motivated these communities ensured they would remain connected. Hence his desire for something that the different churches in the different ethnic and linguistic communities across a diverse empire could identify and own.

Drawing together these three elements in the context of early Christianity, it becomes clear that creeds began as simple summaries of faith to enable new Christians to join the community and *declare* that faith publicly. They emerged out of the need to *defend* Christian faith from its detractors and to *define* the shape of that faith as it grew.

Orthodoxy and Scripture

Creeds emerged during the period in which what became the New Testament was slowly emerging out of the many documents circulating around the early Church. A book, or more correctly a library of books written over a period of a thousand years with nearly 800,000 words, is a very long and complex text. The need was felt for some kind of orientation, a brief guide to what is most important in it so that those who heard the message of Scripture didn't get fixated on tiny details and miss the large and most crucial ideas and themes. As Nicholas Lash puts it, 'What Scripture says at length, the Creed says briefly.'[11]

The rise of Gnosticism and use of the emerging Christian Scriptures raised questions about authority and interpretation, which is why Irenaeus in particular focuses a great deal on the authority of the Church in the interpretation of the Bible. These early theologians did not believe that the Church conferred authority on these texts, but rather recognized an authority that was already there. Remember Irenaeus: 'the Church, having received this preaching, and this faith . . . carefully preserves it. She also believes these points of doctrine . . . and she proclaims them, and teaches them, and hands them down, with perfect harmony.'[12]

Besides needing a summary, some criterion was needed to discern what was a particularly *Christian* reading of Scripture as opposed to one that was an inauthentic and misleading reading of the text, in the light of the overall sense of there being an apostolic tradition going back to those who knew Jesus in the flesh.

Robert Jenson argues that the creeds should be viewed as the right 'critical theory' for the reading of Scripture.[13] Critical theory is an approach to texts that tries to discern what is going on under the surface, what the hidden dynamics and interests at play within the text are. This is often viewed from a particular perspective, so we get feminist theory, post-colonialist theory, queer theory and so on. These give a set of instructions or a lens through which to read a text to enable us to understand its underlying dynamics and how it reads from a given perspective. While these approaches can give valuable perspectives, we might ask what the primary critical theory the Church should use to read Scripture is, to discern what is going on in Scripture or even to understand what God might be doing in it. Jenson's answer (and Irenaeus thought something similar) is that the set of instructions is not left to individual Christians to make up, but is found in the creeds. Creeds therefore function as this kind of guide, the lens through which the Church is to read its Scriptures to discern the nature of the God revealed in them and what they say about the world, its future and so on.

Those who composed the creeds depended on more than human wisdom, usually invoking the guidance of the Spirit. The texts surrounding the composition of the Nicene Creed, for example, make it clear that the Nicene Fathers placed themselves under the guidance of the Holy Spirit for their work. The expectation was that, when leaders of the church met together in Council, they were guided by the Holy Spirit and that the God of whom they were speaking was at the same time guiding their processes of discernment. Of course, the sixteenth-century Reformers insisted that councils can make mistakes, and this was recognized even in the Patristic era. The Council at Ephesus in 449, for example, became known as the 'Robber Council' because its teaching was reversed by a later gathering in the same city two years later. The presence of the Spirit was invoked but could not be presumed. In a sense, it could only be discerned retrospectively through the longevity and enduring character of the teaching of each council and the Church's discernment of its faithfulness to Scripture over time.

Creeds therefore do not replace the Scriptures that emerged over these times, but they relate directly to it, both summarizing it and being confirmed by it. Creeds summarize Scripture (the Nicene Creed uses 175 words in the original Greek to summarize the 800,000 words of the Bible) yet send us back to Scripture to fill in the details of what they briefly mention. They can be compared to the introduction to a book that points out to the reader what to look for, why it was written and how to approach it. The introduction doesn't mean you can dispense with the book (and you can read the book without the introduction), but reading the book is helped by an introduction that points the reader in the right direction.

Scripture needs creeds and creeds need Scripture. A Christian reader might think he or she can do without creeds, but they inevitably shape a Christian reading of the text. A Christian cannot read the story of creation in Genesis 1 without reflecting on the Trinity, with the reference to the Father creating, the Spirit brooding over the waters, and recalling what John's Gospel says about all things being created through Christ. We read the story of the baptism of Jesus with the same framework of the Father sending the Spirit upon the Son.[14] Yet at the same time, when we recite the creeds, they keep reminding us of the scriptural grounds for what they say. This was particularly true during the period of the formation of the creeds, as any familiarity with the Christian literature of the fourth and fifth centuries will show.

The nature of creeds

It was only later, in the course of the various theological and especially Christological controversies of the fourth and fifth centuries, that creeds really began to become tests of formal orthodoxy. As Frances Young puts it:

> [Creeds] are not 'Articles of Belief' or a system of doctrine, but rather confessions summarising the Christian story, or affirmations of the three characters in the story. They tell who God is and what he has done. They invite the convert to make that story and that affirmation his or her own.[15]

That word 'confession' is important. Creeds were sometimes called 'confessions', and this element of confessing the faith publicly was a vital aspect of the function of creeds in the early Church.

John Webster points out that creeds 'properly emerge out of one of the primary and defining activities of the church, the act of confession.'[16] Confession, he argues, is a response to the overwhelming generosity of God in Jesus Christ so that, for example, when St Paul recalls the 'surpassing grace' of God, his instinctive response is to confess 'Thanks be to God for his indescribable gift!' (2 Cor. 9.15). If, so far, we have been exploring the context that shaped the emergence of creeds, we now get to the heart of the instinct towards credal confession in Christian faith. They are not a rigid attempt to fix doctrine in aspic, or an attempt to close down further thinking but, in essence, they are part of the Church's response to the surprising and wonderful initiative of God in revealing himself in Jesus Christ and the gift of salvation. They are an instinctive cry of praise, worship and confession. As Webster puts it, 'confession is more a matter of astonishment than an attempt at closure.'[17]

Divine grace is an interruption to our normal expectations of how life goes. It cuts across our normal expectations of what we deserve and owe and so it constantly surprises us. Confessions, as responses to this grace, always therefore cut across the values and norms of a world in rebellion against God. They will often have a controversial, contested and, to a certain extent, combative character. Confessions and creeds have often held distinct political overtones. In the Reformation period, for example, the Augsburg Confession, the doctrinal foundation of what became Lutheranism, was a defiant statement of Protestant faith in the face of the Catholic empire and was forged in resistance to attempts to clamp down on the spread of vernacular Bibles and Lutheran ideas. In more recent times, the Barmen Confession, mainly drafted by Karl Barth, was a bold statement of Christian faith that specifically aimed to refute Nazi ideology in 1930s Germany. It is often missed, however, that even our more familiar creeds have these audacious overtones of political and personal conviction. As Jaroslav Pelikan put it:

> The orthodox formulas of the Creed of Nicaea . . . confessing the 'one God' to be 'the Father all powerful, maker of all things both seen and unseen' and the Son of God to be 'one in being with the Father', can be taken to imply the radical subordination of all political authority, including even that

of an orthodox Christian emperor, to the lordship of God the Father and of his coequal Son.[18]

Credal orthodoxy puts any leader, ecclesiastical or political, firmly in their place.

I remember an occasion in the chapel of an Anglican theological College. A visiting preacher delivered a sermon of somewhat dubious Christological orthodoxy and questionable exegesis. Immediately after the sermon came the Nicene Creed, and I have never heard the creed belted out with such defiance and volume as on that occasion. It was perhaps a little over-combative, but it did make me think that this, at least in part, is what creeds were for. They were never meant to be bland lists of items of belief to be ticked off, but were meant to be deliberately controversial and provocative statements made not just in the context of church but in the context of wider debates as to what really mattered in life.

Creeds are instinctive cries of praise. They are also acts of allegiance. The Apostles' Creed begins with one simple word: *Credo* ('I believe'). The Greek text of the Niceno-Constantinopolitan Creed of 381 starts with the plural *pisteuōmen* ('we believe'). The word 'belief' has come to indicate for us a kind of passive intellectual assent. It can feel like an answer to the vaguely interesting question whether you believe there to be a God. Of course, it's quite possible to answer 'yes' or 'no' to that question but for that to mean very little in terms of the rest of your life. Belief in God might be an interesting personal opinion, but can actually make little difference to anything else. In the creeds, however, this one word is a dramatic declaration indicating both loyalty and defiance.

Nicholas Lash captures this sense of personal immersion and commitment that these words convey: '"I believe"' does not express an opinion, however well founded or firmly held, concerning God's existence. It promises that life and love, mind, heart, and all my actions, are set henceforward steadfastly on God, and God alone.'[19]

At their baptism, those early Christian converts were asked questions about whether they believed in God: Father, Son and Holy Spirit. Lash compares this to the questions asked of a bride and bridegroom about whether they will commit to the other. In the context of the creeds, saying 'I (or we) believe' and committing to Christian orthodoxy is not a statement of a random belief in the existence of a supreme being, but a personal act of commitment which, certainly in the context of early Christianity or in certain parts of the world today, could cost you your life.

Creeds, therefore, are bold pledges of allegiance, like passionate chants at a football match or the singing of a national anthem. They define us when we say them and they are the distinctive means by which Christians navigate the world. Perhaps in the context of Christendom, the recitation of creeds became a sign of conformity, the test of belonging to a broadly Christian culture. In the world of post-Christendom, however, their true character is revealed again as bold statements of a different reality. They are not a sign that Christians are good citizens, fully 'on message' and in step with the world but, as John Webster puts it, a declaration that 'we are properly out of step with the world and therefore trying to keep pace with God'.[20]

The meaning of orthodoxy

If creeds help define orthodoxy, their controversial and confessional character involving personal allegiance begins to frame an understanding of the nature of orthodoxy itself.

The word 'orthodoxy' originally derives from two Greek words: 'orthos' and 'doxa'. Orthos means 'straight', 'right' or 'true'. When joined to another word, it signifies the right way to do something, or putting things right. So, for example, when you need your teeth straightening, you go to an orthodontist, a specialist in the branch of dentistry that relates to aligning or straightening teeth or jaws. We also have orthopaedic surgeons, whose job it is to ensure our bones, muscles, joints, ligaments, tendons and nerves all work well together, allowing us to move freely and to remain active.[21] Orthotics is a medical specialism that deals with the provision and use of artificial devices such as splints and braces to help broken or twisted bones or limbs to heal well. In all of these cases, the prefix 'ortho-' indicates the straightening of something that has become broken or malformed. It pulls things into shape, enabling our bodies to grow in a healthy and flexible way.

The other word in 'orthodoxy' is '*doxa*', which can be defined as brightness, fame or renown. The associated Greek verb, *doxadzō* simply means to praise, glorify or worship. So, putting it simply, if *orthodontics* is getting teeth straight, *orthodoxy* is getting worship straight. Nicholas Lash puts it like this: 'To say the creed is to perform an act which has one object: right worship of the mystery of God.'[22]

Now, this has been particularly true in the Eastern tradition of Christianity where orthodoxy is not primarily about correct opinions or ideas but is related first and foremost to worship.[23] Nicholas Zernov comments:

> The word Orthodox in the West is understood as 'correct' or 'generally approved' and is applied especially to doctrine. In Greek, *doxa* stands for both teaching and worship. In Slavonic, Orthodoxy is rendered by the word *Pravoslavie*, meaning 'true glory'. When a Russian, Serb or Bulgarian calls himself an Orthodox Christian he means he belongs to the community which praises and glorifies God in the right spirit.[24]

The question of whether Eastern or Western churches worship God aright can be left to one side for the moment, but this Eastern perspective is in itself a more helpful and constructive way to view the nature of orthodoxy. The tendency in the West to define orthodoxy as 'right thinking' or 'correct opinion' is not only etymologically mistaken but can also lead to the kind of dull, restrictive, oppressive versions of orthodoxy that we touched on earlier. In Romans 12, when St Paul appeals to the Christians in Rome not to be conformed to this world but to be 'renewed in their minds', the purpose of this intellectual renewal is described in two ways. It is 'so that you may discern what is the will of God – what is good and acceptable and perfect' and so that they might offer their bodies to God 'which is your spiritual worship' (Rom. 12.1–2). In other words, right thinking and right language are closely bound up with right action and right worship, rather than being ends in themselves.

The purpose of orthodoxy is not to get our ideas straight, it is to get our worship right. This mattered because these early Christian theologians recognized that worship shapes us. The words that we tend to repeat to others and to ourselves regularly, whether in prayers, liturgies, songs, sermons, or even in the websites we read or the social media we follow, tend to gradually form our minds and hearts and therefore our behaviour. The words we speak and listen to matter.

Readers who examine the processes that led to the formation of the creeds often come away bemused by the vehemence with which these theologians argued over what appeared to be minuscule differences in phraseology. The fourth-century Cappadocian bishop St Basil the Great, for example, in his work *On the Holy Spirit*, goes into great detail to establish the correct prepositions to be used when referring to the relationship between the Father, Son and Spirit. He asks whether we should refer to the Spirit as the one 'with whom' or 'through whom' thanks and glory are given, or whether we should glorify the Father and the Son 'with', or 'in' the Holy Spirit. The reason why such precision is necessary is a little like taking a picture through a long zoom lens. The photographer will twist the lens with the finest gradations so that he or she is able to see the subject of the photograph with as much clarity as possible before taking the picture. If the lens is only slightly off focus, the picture will come out blurred and indistinct. The full beauty of the object photographed can only be seen when it is observed with absolute clear sight.

Gregory of Nyssa, Basil's elder brother, is typical of many early Christian approaches to worship. For him, worship was not just saying words in church but gazing on the beauty of God so that, gradually, we are changed into the nature of the one we gaze upon: 'those who look towards the true God receive within themselves the characteristics of the divine nature.'[25] Worship is spiritual formation, and human nature 'cannot become beautiful until it draws nearer to the Beautiful and becomes transformed by the image of the divine beauty'.[26] If this is anywhere near true, getting our words right in worship matters.

Yet there is something even more going on. St Basil, for example, was concerned that his congregation in Caesarea in Asia Minor were a little too prone to join in the local popular habit of drinking contests and the inevitable rowdiness and destructive behaviour that it led to. The teachers Basil opposed argued that when the Scriptures spoke of the Holy Spirit, what they really referred to was a kind of 'ministering spirit' sent by God – in other words, a created angelic messenger. By insisting that the Spirit who was at work in them was not just another kind of angel but fully divine, to be worshipped alongside ('with') the Father and the Son, he was encouraging these Christians tempted to prove their virility by their capacity for alcohol that the instinct from the Spirit that they sensed in their minds to avoid such behaviour was not just another random impulse or a bit of useful advice but the work of *God himself* in their hearts and lives. This teaching was an encouragement that if they wanted more of God's work in their lives shaping them into the image of Jesus, who is the true picture of God in human life, they needed to be free of the swings of emotion that came with getting drunk, to make room for the divine Spirit to be at work in them to bring about stability, reliability and, ultimately, happiness. It was helping them to see that they needed to make a choice between the spirits – divine or alcoholic. If they had these thoughts burned into their memories, it would be an extra incentive to duck out of the drinking bouts and avoid the inevitable broken promises and hurtful words (not to mention the hangovers) they would inevitably lead to. True doctrine, proper orthodoxy, would lead to good, healthy lives.

In a very insightful book, Ellen Charry demonstrates how this aspect of Christian orthodoxy works. She shows how for figures such as St Paul, Athanasius, Augustine, Anselm, Julian of Norwich and John Calvin, the point of orthodox teaching or doctrine (even in these Western theologians!) was not simply correct opinion for its own sake, but the development of virtue, the living of good, healthy human lives. For her, these classic theologians 'held that knowing and loving God is the mechanism of choice for forming excellent character and promoting genuine happiness'.[27] As David Steinmetz put it, commenting on the cover of the book:

> It would have astonished Athanasius and Basil to have been told by theologians from our century that the doctrines of the Trinity and the two natures of Christ were abstract metaphysical puzzles, devoid of pastoral intent and divorced from human life. The whole point of these doctrines was after all, to explain how ordinary people could participate in the life of God.

The reason why we need to pay attention to what is orthodox is not so much that we can sit back, resting content that our opinions of God and each other are correct and that we would be sure to pass some heavenly examination on doctrine, but primarily that we might live well. The purpose of credal orthodoxy is not to police opinion but to give us a map to enable us to explore the island we live on, to enable us to think clearly, to live well in it and to worship right.

Conclusion

Creeds emerged through the early Christian context of persecution from the need to confess the faith both within the Church and outside it, and from the debates about the identity of Christian faith in those early centuries. At their heart, however, they are an instinctive response to the grace and mercy of God in Jesus Christ. As such, they are far more than a mere list of items to be assented to or a restrictive straitjacket on thinking. They are statements of personal allegiance and even of defiance to a world that is a long way away from the purposes of its Creator. The orthodoxy that creeds point to is therefore not just about correct opinions but embraces intellectual belief, ethical decision making, a healthy life and Christian worship.

But how did the creeds actually shape these early Christians and how might they shape us today? The next chapter begins to explore these vital questions by looking at what they say about the world we live in.

2
Creator of heaven and earth

Where does morality come from? And why do we disagree so vehemently about ethics, politics and religion? It's a question asked by the social psychologist Jonathan Haidt, in his book *The Righteous Mind*.[1] One influential theory is that we reason our way to good ethical decisions, carefully weighing up the advantages and disadvantages, the rights and wrongs of particular ethical dilemmas. It sounds sensible but has one flaw: it is wrong.

Haidt argues that the real driver of our ethical decision making is not so much reason but instinct. Reasoning then comes in to justify judgements made mainly by intuition. Reason, he says, acts like a good lawyer doing what it can to argue the case of our intuitions and instincts, although on occasion refusing to go along with requests and suggesting another way forward.

What then determines the direction in which our instincts nudge us? For Haidt, that is largely determined by the stories we believe about the world. For example, generalizing wildly, social conservatives tend to intuit the world as a dangerous and risky place, so humans need constraints and limits to curb threats to our wellbeing and ensure a healthy way of living. Progressives tend to enjoy novelty, change and new experiences, thinking the world is basically a rich and exciting place to explore, that people are generally good and tend to flourish when constraints are removed.

Stories matter. They matter because the stories we believe tend to determine what we do and what we value. The idea that we are all simply rationalistic creatures, 'following the science' is just an illusion. The stories we listen to and believe to be true are, in fact, more influential on us than supposedly rational arguments. The ethicist Gilbert Meilaeder writes:

successful moral education requires a community which does not hesitate to inculcate virtue in the young, which does not settle for the discordant opinions of alternative visions of the good, which worries about what the stories of its poets teach.[2]

That's why those first two words of the creeds are so important: 'I believe'. Find out what someone believes about where they came from, what the world is, who they are and how to successfully navigate a way through life and that story will largely determine how they act and conduct their lives. It's why Martin Luther argued that everything rests on faith. Everything depends upon the stories and people we believe, the promises we trust.

The problem is that, for most of us, that story is never fully articulated. It's common to say these days that there is no common narrative in Western cultures, no overarching story that holds everyone together. That may be so, but there are some stories that are fairly widely held. For example, the political philosopher Patrick Deneen argues that underneath the 'culture wars' between left and right, progressives and conservatives, there is, in fact, a fundamental agreement. Regardless of who happens to be in power at any one time, modern liberal democracies see us all as autonomous individuals who should ideally be free from the constraints of duty or the demands of others and instead set at liberty to follow our desires. The only difference is that the right sees the market and minimum state interference as the key to enabling these personal freedoms, whereas the left sees state control and regulation as the way those freedoms will be established and safeguarded.[3]

Another version of this story is articulated by the German sociologist Hartmut Rosa, who argues that, while we have a huge variety of versions of the 'good life' (at least in Western societies) we do, in fact, have fairly widespread agreement on the preconditions needed for that life:

Modern society might not have an answer to what the good life is or what it consists in, but it has a very clear-cut answer to what the preconditions for living a good life are, and what to do for meeting them. 'Secure the resources you might need for living your dream' (whatever that might be) has become the overruling rational imperative of modernity.[4]

Those necessary resources tend to be things like money, personal rights, influential friends, health, and the knowledge that comes through education. The more of those you can get, the more likely you are to be able to achieve your dream and the happier you will be. Western societies and governments are therefore judged on how available, accessible and attainable they make those resources.

If these are the stories we believe, the results that follow – the competitive, polarized nature of society, the primacy of consumption with the knock-on effects that has on our planet, the loss of a sense of community and the resultant epidemic of loneliness – is not at all surprising.

Stories matter. And that is why creeds matter.

The story in the creeds

We are essentially story-telling and story-believing creatures. The Enlightenment search for universal foundations for knowledge has run into trouble and, as a result, in the words of the sociologist Christian Smith, 'what we have come to see is that at bottom *we are all really believers*'.[5] Narratives are our way of organizing and structuring reality and identity. Smith argues that in the modern world there are a number of stories that we tell ourselves and that give us a sense of order in the world. There are, for example, the narratives of capitalist prosperity, progressive socialism, Islamic resurgence, expressive romanticism or scientific enlightenment. None of these stories can be proved to be absolutely true but, depending on which one we believe, they determine the way we see the world and act within it.

The classic Christian creeds that summarize Christian orthodoxy tell a story. If much of Western culture effectively says, 'I believe I am an autonomous individual who seeks a good life for myself and my friends and family through acquiring enough money, contacts, and knowledge to pursue my dream of making the world a better place', or something along those lines, Christians start in a different place: 'We believe in one God, the Father, the Almighty, maker of heaven and earth, of all that is, seen and unseen.'

The creeds tell a story that starts at the very beginning with God and creation, proceeds to focus on a series of historical events in the first century AD concerning Jesus of Nazareth, named as the Jewish *Christos* or Messiah, as the central clue to the whole story, continues with his resurrection and Ascension, and then looks forward to the end of all things, concluding, 'We look for the resurrection of the dead, and the life of the world to come.'

This is the story that we Christians believe about ourselves and about the world. If Jonathan Haidt is right (and there are many Christian thinkers from Augustine to Pascal and contemporary theologians such as James K. A. Smith[6] who would similarly argue for the limits to reason as the main driver of human action), then this is the story that, to the extent that we believe it, will shape our lives for better or worse. In the last chapter, we saw creeds as confessional statements, bold assertions of loyalty and even defiance against a world that believes other stories. They tell a story from the beginning to the end of time, but the central character in that story is not us, it is God. To say the creed is to state boldly that I believe and put my ultimate trust not in the market, nor the state, nor even in myself but in the God who is Father, Son and Holy Spirit.

The main Christian creeds are the three 'ecumenical' or 'worldwide' creeds accepted by most Western Christian denominations: the Apostles' Creed which, despite its name, does not go back to the Apostles but has its origins in second-century Rome; the Niceno-Constantinopolitan Creed finalized in 381; and the much longer and more complex Athanasian Creed, which is attributed to Athanasius but probably dates from around the sixth century.

In this book, we will focus mainly on the Nicene Creed as a key summary of Christian orthodoxy, for several reasons:

First, it is the only creed that is accepted across the three major families of Christian faith in the world: Orthodox, Catholic and Protestant.[7]

Second, it is the fruit of long pondering, praying, discussing and arguing over many years leading up to the Council of Nicaea in 325 AD and long afterwards. Recent scholarship has shown how contested the Christology of the council was in the years which followed.[8] Other subsequent councils issued alternative creeds and, from 357–360, the Nicene creed was officially replaced across the empire, with use of its controversial term *homoousios* – the idea that the Son was 'of one being' with the Father – banned for a while before eventually being affirmed again at the Council of Constantinople in 381. These debates, however, strangely confirm rather than deny the value of the Nicene Creed. Of course, imperial politics, theological argument and charismatic personalities all had an influence on the story, yet the fact that this long and heated discussion resulted in the adoption of this one creed that remains in place 1,700 years later says something about its durability and its capacity to animate and unite the Christian community across the world.

Much could be said about the creeds. However, in this chapter, I want to introduce one particular aspect of this story through the lens of the first line of the Nicene Creed. Thinking of a generous orthodoxy, we are invited to imagine an orthodoxy that is generous in the sense of being large, expansive and capacious. We sometimes talk about being given a 'generous portion' of pudding or someone who exhibits generosity as 'big-hearted'. I want to show how generous Christian orthodoxy gives us a bigger picture of the world than any secular vision can offer. It enables a proper thinking inside, not outside, the box because the box is a lot bigger than we think.

A bigger world

Charles Taylor, in his magisterial *A Secular Age*, has written of the 'immanent frame' of secularity.[9] The premodern world, whether pagan, Christian or inspired by other religious visions, thought of this world as a sign and pointer to a transcendent world beyond itself. Societies were grounded in this broader cosmic order and this world was an enchanted world, open to all kinds of things that we cannot explain. A secular age is not, as is often assumed, what gets left behind when you take God and the transcendent out of the picture, but it is an entirely new construction, a different view of the world that replaces the worldview of premodern people. The modern view of the world is bounded like a picture in a frame – a frame of immanence, which generally *excludes* the transcendent as a part of reality. The frame of a picture both includes and excludes. It includes whatever is found within the frame but excludes all that is outside it. The mental operating system of a secular age often assumes a 'closed world structure', a picture of the world that is confined to what can be scientifically proven or rationally explained.

Christian orthodoxy gives us a bigger, more expansive, generous and much more interesting picture of the world than secularity, one that leads us to a way of life which is healthier and, in its own way more generous and generative. It is a vision that requires an expanded imagination, which has in the past inspired some of the greatest works of art and architecture in human history.

The creeds speak about God as the Creator of all that is 'seen and unseen'. This includes what most people in the world intuitively know: that there are all kinds of unseen realities. What can be seen, touched and measured is not the whole story. A purely materialist world is really a very small world. It has no room for notions such as grace, holiness, the existence of angels or the possibility of the miraculous. Of course, we have to beware of credulity and fanciful claims, but look closely at the detailed architecture of a Medieval cathedral and you will see this expanded world just assumed in a way that modern, closed-minded materialists find hard to imagine.

This is a vision of the world that is just too big to fit into modern secular ways of thinking. It can be done, of course, but that is to reduce Christian faith to something much less interesting. It is perhaps what the Church has so often done in recent years, which is why Christian faith seems so dull and unappealing to so many people. We have so often tried to reinterpret Christian faith within the immanent frame rather than starting with the expansive, rich vision of reality given by the creeds themselves.

The Father Almighty, Creator of heaven and earth

The creeds begin with belief in 'God the Father Almighty, Maker of heaven and earth' (Apostles') or 'one God, the Father, the Almighty, maker of heaven and earth, of all that is, seen and unseen' (Nicene).

They begin, therefore, with the idea that what we see around us is not just nature but creation. It is not just 'what happens to be there', the accidental outcome of a series of chemical reactions at the beginning of time, but the work of a cosmic artist or Creator.

At the time when Christianity burst on to the scene in the first century AD, there were a number of beliefs about how this world came to be. Aristotle believed that the universe was eternal. Stoics believed that fire was the basic element out of which all things were made and that *logos* (reason), permeated and brought order to what was originally chaotic and disordered. Epicureans believed that everything that exists is made up of atoms that come together into bodies and then disperse when they die, and that the gods show no great interest in human life so we are not to worry too much about them either. Platonists believed the world to be the product of eternal Mind, or the demiurge, ordering pre-existent matter. All of them believed in some way or another that creation is the reordering of material that existed beforehand.

Many of the various Gnostic groups – those strange, complex gatherings that arose alongside what became orthodox Christian teaching – also believed in creation out of pre-existent matter, physical material that tied our souls to the earth, so that salvation was the escape from the body and not its renewal or resurrection. When Irenaeus, in the second century, started to refute the Gnostics, he, along with other early Christian theologians such as Tertullian, began to actively promote the radical idea, derived from the Bible, that it was not *matter* that was eternal, but God.[10] God created the world *ex nihilo* (out of nothing). In the beginning, there was not eternal, disordered chaotic matter, just God. This was an idea that had begun to gain traction in Hellenistic Judaism and was implicit in the New Testament in texts such as St Paul's description of the God 'who gives life to the dead and calls into existence the things that do not exist' (Rom. 4.17).

This was a belief that distinguished Christianity from the Greek philosophies of the time[11] and carried a number of key implications. By making matter temporal not eternal, it might have seemed that Christianity was diminishing the significance of the physical world. Yet, in fact, the opposite is the case.

Creation and moral formation

We have already met Basil the Great, Bishop of Caesarea in Asia Minor in the fourth century, one of the most significant of the early Christian Fathers and who had an influence on the eventual form of the Niceno-Constantinopolitan Creed of 381 AD. He preached a series of sermons that eventually appeared under the title of the *Hexaemeron* (a reference to the six days of creation), which illustrates the vision of creation behind the creed. Pagans believed that nothing existed before formless matter and that therefore *'nothing* governed or ruled the universe, and that all was given up to chance,'[12] hence the anxious uncertainty of pagan worship, which sought by whatever means possible – sacrifices, libations, donations to the temples of the gods – to bring order to and resist the underlying chaos of the world. This chaos – the disasters of flood, volcanic eruption or social chaos – felt uncomfortably close in the ancient world and there was little defence against it as it threatened to engulf the world again.

Instead, Basil points out, the world emerged not out of pre-existent matter or chaotic disorder but from one who is

> Goodness without measure, a worthy object of love for all beings endowed with reason, the beauty the most to be desired, the origin of all that exists, the source of life, intellectual light, impenetrable wisdom, it is He who in the beginning created heaven and earth.[13]

The foundation of the world is not chaos that always threatens to overwhelm us but goodness, beauty and wisdom, which is waiting to be found if we dig deep enough. This, fundamentally, is a world of grace.

As a result, for Basil, the world is not a fearsome place with disaster waiting around every corner but a place of wisdom, learning and moral formation: 'The world is a work of art displayed for the beholding of all people; to make them know him who created it.'[14] Every created thing has a meaning and purpose: 'Not a single thing has been created without reason, not a single thing is useless.'[15] Basil shows a fascination with the intricate details of the natural world, like a fourth-century David Attenborough, although he sees the world not as the product of impersonal evolutionary forces but as the creation of a good and wise God. For him, the world is best understood not in the light of rationalistic scientific exploration of the internal workings of biology and physics but as shedding light on the wisdom of God and the moral life.

Basil sees nature as full of meaning. Plants that grow, flower into bloom and then die are reminders of youth, old age and the inevitability of death. A vine is a picture of human life and desire that grows and bears fruit but only by being pruned and disciplined. The vastness and peace of a calm sea on the one hand enables travel and trade, making possible the redistribution of goods that bless the poor with the supply of what they lack but, on the other, it is a picture of the Church 'where the voices of men, of children, and women, arise in our prayers to God, mingling and resounding like the waves which beat upon the shore.'[16] The moon that waxes and wanes is a symbol of human inconstancy compared to the constancy of the sun. This is reading nature through the lens of the gospel rather than the other way round. Basil suggests that, in the original creation, roses originally had no thorns, yet thorns were added to the rose as a reminder that sorrow is near to pleasure and that sin lies waiting near to us at all times.

Some of Basil's scientific guesses sound quite curious to us now. He is no proto-biologist and his understanding of the make-up of the natural world reflects the science of his day. Yet it is a reading of nature that is not fundamentally dependent on that science, or ours, for that matter. It is a reading of creation as holding a whole extra layer of meaning over and above the biological. It is a moral reading of nature as a guide to the wise living of human life. More than that, however, it sees nature as a gift that points us to the order and wisdom that lie at the very heart of reality.

This is not like the later deistic 'natural theology' that derives the designer from the design of the universe. It does not seek to prove the existence of God from nature. In fact, like the Bible, Basil is not interested in proving the existence of God at all. Instead, he simply assumes the existence of the God revealed in Christ and the Scriptures and describes the world in the light of that knowledge. As in the creed, God comes at the beginning and not the end of the argument. This is a view of the world as created through the Word and bearing the stamp of Christ who is the 'wisdom of God' (1 Cor. 1.30). The post-Enlightenment view of the world as a place of benevolent order designed for the well-being of humankind was an anthropocentric view of the world that posited a remote and distant God overseeing a machine that functioned without his ongoing involvement, like Paley's famous image of the watch and the watchmaker. This is different. The order found within the world is not so much a scientific order as a moral one. This moral order is not, as it were, found for the first time through observation of nature, but the order found there confirms the moral order found within the Scriptures and in the revelation of Christ. After all, the *Hexaemeron* is a series of sermons on the text of Genesis 1 rather than a documentary of the natural world.

This is an educational reading of creation that is not unscientific (even if his science is undeveloped) but goes beyond that to envelop a wider range of meaning. He looks into the detail of the natural world to inspire wonder and cultivate gratitude: 'I want creation to fill you with so much admiration that everywhere, wherever you may be, the least plant may bring to you the clear remembrance of the Creator.'[17] This is creation as the teacher of virtue, the natural world as an aid to personal and spiritual formation. For Basil, the world came into being not by accident or as a deistic machine, the product of a remote and disinterested divinity, but for a precise purpose: to school us into knowledge and love of the God who made us, the Father Almighty.

So, the tree outside my window is no longer just a tree, a configuration of organic matter that grew from a random seed into a trunk, branches and leaves, but is a gift to me in this present moment as I see it and rejoice in its colour, size and longevity. It carries a personal meaning as gift from a good and generous God in a way that no scientific explanation could ever say. Yet, more than this, it has the potential to carry meaning as a picture of faithfulness and steadiness as it remains rooted within the ground, the reality of seasons of life when the time is right for withdrawal and protection from the harsh winds of winter in preparation for later flourishing and fruitfulness, as it grows and flowers every year in the spring and summer.

This is not to oppose this reading to a scientific one. To repeat the point above, Basil happens to be interested in the science of his day, but this moral and spiritual, even Christological reading of nature is independent of that science. This extra layer of meaning that creation brings is independent of and quite compatible with an understanding of biology and physics. It can embrace and fully value that scientific understanding yet gives a bigger and fuller view of the world.

The personal origins of the world

To go back to the creed, the statement that it was the 'Father Almighty' who made heaven and earth indicates the personal and even parental origins of the world in which we live. This planet that is our home did not emerge from impersonal chemical forces, chance events at the beginning of time, or as an accidental offshoot of war between the gods as the Babylonian myths had it. Instead, it was given as a completely gratuitous, unnecessary and yet generous gift from a good Father. Because the world derives only from God the Father Almighty and not from some faceless, pre-existent matter that has no regard for us whatsoever, it is a place where we can feel at home because it is provided for us and given as a gift. It is what Robert Jenson has called a 'drastically revisionary metaphysics . . . we exist and exist as we do because God determines that we shall, and that is all there is to be said'.[18]

We might then ask: who is this Father who is the maker of all things? After all, our own experience of fathers may or may not be particularly good or positive so a good deal hangs on this question. The answer that the creed gives us, to anticipate the next article a few lines further down, is that he is first and foremost not our Father but the Father of the Son. The Father of Jesus Christ is the Creator of heaven and earth. This immediately brings into play the relationships within the Trinitarian life of God that we will look at in due course: this is the Father who 'loves the Son and has placed all things in his hands' (John 3.35). It begins to fill out the nature of the God who created the world, the Father from whom the Son is begotten and the Spirit proceeds.

Paganism, unsurprisingly for a system of worship grounded in philosophies that taught the eternity of matter, was a form of nature worship with its sacred groves, its worship of the 'gods', and its fascination with astrology and the manipulation of magical powers and forces for one's own advantage. Seeing nature as in some sense eternal, existing alongside God, discouraged any sense of examining that nature to understand how it works. A culture that views a particular mountain as the sacred abode of the gods does not allow mere mortals to trespass on its slopes, let alone attack it with geological hammers.

Many have therefore pointed out that a combination of the doctrine of creation *ex nihilo* and the idea that it was created from the Father through the divine *Logos* was precisely the kind of metaphysic that made modern science possible.[19] Refusing to see the physical world as divine or eternal but as created in time, by drawing a strict line between Creator and creation, it became possible to analyse and begin to understand the inner physical workings of that creation. A different metaphysics enabled a new kind of physics.

Nicene orthodoxy also sees the Son of the Father as integral to creation: 'through him all things were made'. This says that *logos*, or reason, is built into it at every point. The world has a pattern, a predictable, coherent form. It was not ruled by pure chance or random necessity but had its own rationality that could be studied and understood. Basil is a fascinating example, from many centuries before the rise of modern science, of a Christian whose faith gives him a deep fascination for the inner workings of the natural world while seeing that there is more to the world than just an understanding of how it works physically.

Implicit within the doctrine of creation *ex nihilo* and brought into being through the *Logos* as described in the creeds is a narrative that dissolves the common idea of warfare between science and religion. As Alister McGrath puts it, 'a Christian conceptual framework, within which science could flourish, is clearly part of the context against which the scientific revolution emerged.'[20]

Why care for creation?

Even more, the idea that the natural world is, in fact, the creation of a good God gives grounds for its preservation. Climate change is perhaps the greatest threat facing not just human life but life itself on the planet, and no one doubts the need to preserve the black rhino, the baobab tree and the Baltic Sea. When it comes to answering the question of *why* such things are worth preserving, the answers get a little thin.[21]

The cosmology found in the various Babylonian and Greek myths of creation, against which the book of Genesis offers a conscious contrast, saw the world as the result of fallout from warfare in the divine courts. It is an accidental by-product of the violence of the gods, hardly a strong basis on which to argue for its value and intrinsic worth. The Greek epics of Homer and Hesiod saw the world as changing but doing so negatively. The world is degenerating from its original age of gold and there is next to nothing we can do about its decline. Plato saw the world as an imperfect copy of what really mattered, abstract 'Forms' that existed in changeless perfection on some metaphysical plane above us. First-century Gnostics thought our destiny and goal must be to escape this ugly and flawed place to the realm of pure spirit.

None of these really saw the physical world as inherently good and therefore worth preserving. They were either mired in a gloomy pessimism about the future or their optimism was based on escaping the physical universe to enter a spiritual world elsewhere. None of them gave a robust basis for action to preserve the earth. More modern views fare little better. Contemporary scientific atheism is forced to admit that the world came about essentially by accident. It can have no intrinsic meaning or value other than that which we choose to give it. There may be a set of physical laws that shape its emergence, or biological patterns that govern the evolution of life, but its origin lies in meaningless randomness and chance.

Some kind of pragmatic reason is usually given to justify climate action: we need to preserve the earth for our grandchildren. But isn't that just another instrumental reason that suggests creation exists for our benefit rather than being good in itself? Secular humanism, which has to conclude that there is no ultimate meaning, purpose or value intrinsic to the physical world, surely leads to the rather lame conclusion that the only reason we value the earth is because it is the only place we have to live on and we don't want to die. The idea that the earth needs preserving because it is the only home we have is just the kind of anthropocentric view of the world that many environmentalists think got us into this mess in the first place.

In contrast to all of these, Nicene orthodoxy suggests that the physical world around us is fundamentally and irrevocably *good*. This planet is a good thing in itself and it doesn't just exist for us. In fact, it doesn't require human life to make it good because its goodness is derived from its origins in a good and creative God, the Father who looked at it and pronounced it good once and for all (Gen. 1.31). This view gives a thorough grounding for modern ecological concern, giving the universe a value in itself and a future to hope for. It is worth preserving because it is a good thing. Not because it we feel sorry for our descendants, not because we need a place to live but simply because it is worth it.

If this world came into being from the Father, through the Son, under the brooding of the Holy Spirit, then this world suddenly seems bigger, more expansive, more generous. The world not only carries scientific meaning but moral and spiritual meaning as well. In the light of God's self-revelation in Christ and the Scriptures, it can be a source of spiritual wisdom and growth. This perspective gives us a solid basis for both scientific exploration and, as we will see in the next chapter, for artistic creativity. It is an example of how Christian orthodoxy is not only *generous* but *generative* of creative and exploratory thinking. The doctrine of creation *ex nihilo* and the doctrine of the Incarnation provide a grounding for seeing that world as a home full of grace, meaning and sense.

3

The only Son of God

The creeds were the outcome of centuries of reflection within the Church after a seismic and world-shattering event: the coming into the world of Jesus Christ. Christology stands at the very heart of Christian orthodoxy, stretching back and forwards both in time and thought to influence everything. As Karl Barth put it in his own sustained reflection on the Nicene Creed, here 'we pass into the heart of the Christian confession . . . Christology is the touchstone of all knowledge of God in the Christian sense, the touchstone of all theology.'[1]

Nicene politics

The Council of Nicaea was called by Emperor Constantine in 325 AD, mainly to resolve a dispute that had broken out in Alexandria between the bishop, Alexander, and Arius, one of his priests, who had argued that the Word that became incarnate in Christ was created at some point by the Father and therefore not truly eternal. There were, as always, complex politics involved in the condemnation of Arius at the council, the adoption of this particular creed and the decision to include the much-debated word *homoousios*, which asserts that the Son was 'of one being' with the Father.[2]

The politics were by no means resolved by the decision at Nicaea. The on-going story of the subsequent debates between various groups arguing over all this throughout the fourth century and beyond testify to the complexity of these issues and the way in which Nicaea did not resolve them once and for all.[3]

Our contemporary fascination with the hidden stories of history and banished heretics can make us feel that Arianism was the exciting option, an idea too revolutionary to be adopted by the staid and conservative 'orthodox', but the reverse is true. The notion that the Son was as eternal as the father, co-eternal, con-substantial, equal to the Father yet distinct from him, was radical, revolutionary, quite distinct from anything familiar in paganism or Judaism and much harder to get your head around.

It is worth pausing to recognize the revolutionary nature of what happened in Nicaea and the sheer unlikeliness of it. Before then, most second-century theologians held some kind of subordinationist view of the relationship between the Father and the Son, assuming that the Son was in some way inferior to the Father. Arius could therefore claim, with some legitimacy, that he was only restating previous theological positions. Even after Nicaea, throughout the fourth century, these subordinationist instincts made much more sense to pagans coming into the church from the outside. The idea that there was one single God who delegated some of his powers to a couple of assistants – lesser gods as it were – was fairly familiar to pagans influenced by a Neoplatonic view of the world. The idea that God was One, yet within that very oneness were found relationships between three 'persons' – Father, Son and Spirit – was revolutionary and unique in world religion or philosophy both then and now.

As the debate continued in the fourth century, it became clear that what the Fathers of Nicaea had said was, in fact, the logic of Scripture and, tempting as the Arian view or any other formula-tion that preserved the single and undivided oneness of God was, it simply wouldn't do.

Those fractious fourth-century debates did not fundamentally change the Church's decision at Nicaea, even if they did clarify it, especially in the subsequent dogma of Chalcedon in 451 (we will look at the Council of Chalcedon further in Chapter 6). What was at stake in these debates was not just a technical and abstract detail about whether Christ was divine or not but more fundamental issues of the relationship between God and the world and the extent to which God could be known within that world.

If the creeds are a map to reality showing us the contours of the island on which we live, we should expect the Christology of the creed to highlight some key insights and pointers as to what matters. This is exactly what we find. The dense and concise Christology of the Nicene Creed tells us who we are and who God is, safeguards a sense of truth, meaning and representation, and gives a framework for human flourishing.

Relational life

The fairly lengthy part of the creed that focuses on Christology narrates in outline the story of Jesus Christ. It tells of his being begotten by the Father before all time, his birth, death, burial and resurrection. It continues with his Ascension into heaven and his future coming in glory. It doesn't focus much on his life story, his teaching or his miracles but more on his identity and his relationship with God the Father.

The Nicene Creed has been criticized by modern theologians such as Jürgen Moltmann and N. T. Wright for omitting mention of the life, miracles and teaching of Jesus, going straight from birth to death and resurrection. However, this is to miss the essential relationship that we have already noticed between creeds and Scripture. The creeds are not trying to retell the full story but to clarify the true identity of this 'one Lord Jesus Christ' that the Gospels tell of, the one who fed huge crowds, healed the sick and preached the kingdom of God. The creed assumes Scripture as its hinterland, that those who recite it will also be readers of the Gospels, and therefore feels no need to tell the whole story. Instead, it focuses on the key questions of Jesus' identity and his work: that this Jesus was the true Son of the Father and all that he accomplished was 'for us and for our salvation'. It does this because, unless we understand that identity, the details of his ministry don't make sense. Once we do understand that when Jesus heals the sick, feeds the hungry, and gives hope to the poor, this is *God* doing it, these events take on a whole new meaning.

It starts his story not, as most human biographies do, with his birth or by describing his ancestors, but with his eternal generation: he is 'eternally begotten of the Father'. In other words, he was not begotten by the Father in time but in eternity. God is therefore an eternal father in that there was never a time when he was not a father. I happen to be a father, but I am not an eternal father in that there was a time when I was not a father. I became one on a day in November 1986 when our first child was born. My fatherhood is therefore incidental and contingent. It would have been quite possible for me not to be a father at all if I had remained single or not had any children. That, however, is not true of God. He has always been the Father of the Son. His Fatherhood is not incidental or contingent but necessary. His Fatherhood is integral to his very being and identity in a way that is not true of me or any other human father, for that matter.

This was an insight of the third-century theologian Origen.[4] It was a bold and dramatic move that helped decisively shift the Church's language and thought about God in the direction of one who was not an isolated monad but who shared his nature with another, and claimed that the relationship between the Father and the Son was essential to the nature of God.

Yet Origen's own language was unclear and controversial in that, like many Christians of the second and third centuries, he envisaged graded levels of divinity with Christ as necessarily inferior to the Father. For Origen, only the Father was God in the fullest sense of the word and the Son was only divine by participation in the Father. For him, the Son was 'eternally generated' from the Father, like thought proceeding from will or brightness from light, as a necessary link between God and the world. For Origen, the Son was, technically speaking, not God but the image of God. These ambiguities needed clarification and, as Rowan Williams has pointed out, while in the mid-200s, questions and tensions in theology could be lived with, in the early 300s, the newly public role of the Church in the Constantinian empire required these theological debates to find resolution if the Church was to play a vital role in drawing together an increasingly fragmented empire.[5]

We have already seen how the first article of the creed identifies God as the 'Father Almighty'. 'Father' is not a common word for God in the Old Testament yet, for Christians, it becomes *the* central word used in prayer to God. As we saw in the last chapter, 'the Father Almighty' is first and foremost the Father of Jesus Christ the Son, who addressed God in this characteristic way as 'Abba, Father' (Mark 14.36) and who taught his disciples to address God similarly as 'Our Father'. As we shall see in the next chapter, it was 'by the power of the Holy Spirit' that the Incarnation took place – the same Spirit who is worshipped alongside the Father and Son and through whom worship of the Father and Son is possible. The Father is the Father of this particular Son and the Son is identified as the Son of this particular Father. The Spirit, as Augustine frequently put it, is the 'bond of love' between this Father and Son.

This is why it never quite works to replace the credal terms 'Father, Son and Spirit' with terms such as 'Creator, Redeemer and Sustainer'. There is an understandable instinct to try to avoid the gender-specific language of 'Father' and 'Son' yet, for better or worse, we don't have any personal language that is not gender-specific one way or the other.[6] In any case, 'Creator, Redeemer and Sustainer' focuses attention on tasks rather than relationships and suggests three independent beings who could, in theory, do their assigned roles without the others. It doesn't carry the essential idea of the relationships between the persons that credal Trinitarian language maintains.[7]

The Christian tradition has usually maintained that, in the life of the Trinity, the relations precede the persons. In other words, each person of the Trinity is defined not by its own individuality or by some inner essence of the self (as we tend to think about ourselves in the individualistic West) but by its relation to the others. 'Creator, Redeemer and Sustainer' implies that what really matters about each person of the Trinity is their job, their distinct uniqueness and role, which arises more from a set of assumptions deeply rooted in modern expressive individualism than from Christian wisdom.

The language we use to describe God, such as 'Father' or 'Son' (or even terms such 'Judge' or 'Shepherd'), does not suggest that God is like our preconceived ideas of what fathers and sons are. It is the other way round. The prophets repeat over and over again that God is precisely *not* like human shepherds, judges or fathers. It is from God's fatherhood, or Jesus' care for Jerusalem like a mother hen for her chicks (Matt. 23.37) that we learn what good parenting is like. It is divine judgement that teaches us to judge rightly. Our debased ideas of patriarchy are critiqued, not reinforced, by this relational language.

In other words, the creed begins to give us a picture of what human life is meant to be. By pointing back to scriptural language and imagery, it fills in a vision of what a good life is. As Nicholas Lash puts it, 'unlike other judges, God judges justly; unlike other shepherds, God brings back the strayed, binds up the cripples, and strengthens the weak; unlike other fathers, God is like the father in the misnamed parable of the prodigal son'.[8]

The vision of personhood that emerges from the creed flatly contradicts the individualism of so much contemporary culture, the idea that we can save ourselves by becoming free from the restrictions and demands placed upon us by other people, by society or by God. This credal idea of God as Father, Son and Spirit offers us a vision of personhood that is defined not by some inner journey to find out who we really are by looking within ourselves and becoming independent of the demands and expectations of others, but one which is, at its very heart, relational. If the Father is who he is only in relation to the Son, the Son is who he is only in relation to the Father, and the Spirit is the active love that binds the Father and the Son together, and if we are made in the image of this God, then we are only ever persons in relation to others. It is in our commitment to others – friends, work colleagues, marriage partners, children, neighbours – that we are formed as human beings, not by some mysterious process of finding identity in our fluctuating and unstable inner feelings or instincts. We are made not for independence but for interdependence.[9]

It is precisely this independence, this sense that we can create ourselves, that we don't need God or anyone else to be ourselves, that is at the heart of sin. It is the failure to recognize our createdness, dependence and limits, the hubris that thinks we don't need our neighbours and that they don't need us, that destroys communities, sets people over against each other and corrodes mutual respect and trust. A fully Trinitarian idea of personhood binds us to one another and yet does so across our usual divisions because it also relates each person to the one God who made them. As Kierkegaard argued, we love others best when God is the 'middle term' in the relationship.[10] We are not permitted the choice just to love those who are like us, but come under the command to love our neighbour whoever they are. The vision of life we see in the creed has the capacity to rebuild a viable and robust sense of communal life in which we connect with those who are unlike us.

The unknown yet knowable God

Like Origen, Arius believed that the Father alone was transcendent, fully God. Unlike Origen, he did not want to concede that the Son was also eternal. Language that had been rumbling around the Church, also used by his own bishop, implying the Son was as eternal as the Father seemed to Arius to compromise the central biblical insight that God is One and unique. It seemed to imply two Gods in the beginning. For Arius, the one thing that needed to be safeguarded was God's uniqueness and distinctness from creation.

A consequence of the oneness of God was God's unknowability. If God is unique, different, with no analogy or shared nature with anything else, God just stands beyond us, beyond knowledge. He is pure mystery in the sense that nothing significant can be said about him. As Rowan Williams puts it, with reference to one of Arius' own works, 'what is most distinctive in the *Thalia* . . . is the theme of the absolute unknowability of the Father.'[11]

For Arius, the Word was solely connected to God's purpose as Creator. God had brought the Word into being as a means of creating the world, but that Word did not in itself necessarily tell us anything about God. Arius thought of the Word as having been created by God as a kind of mediator through whom he could create the rest of the world yet, as Athanasius later pointed out, if that were true, the Word could not tell us anything reliable about

God himself. It might tell us something about God's will, but not his inner life or identity. By contrast, for Athanasius and the pro-Nicenes, 'what is revealed in the incarnation of the word is the eternal nature of God'.[12]

At the heart of this debate and the central assertion of the Nicene Creed that the Son is *homoousios* – 'of one being' with the Father – is the question of what we are looking at when we look at the Jesus Christ of the Gospels. Are we considering a historical figure that shows us the very best of what human life can be? Is this another (even the best) image of the triumph of the human spirit? Whenever we read the biography of a heroic character from the past, even in our own cynical age that tends to emphasize the frailty and weakness of such figures, we are shown a picture of human capacity and potential. Every biography contains a kind of moral. The unspoken message of any biography is either a warning – that, without due care, the fate of this particular individual could be yours – or a picture of the great feats human beings are capable of given resolve, determination and talent.

Arius' picture of Jesus is an inspiring vision of human potential, an image of what a human being can achieve or endure in the face of intense suffering. However, we are not short of those. Karl Barth pointed out that we are surrounded by all kinds of reminders and revelations of power, beauty and love in the lives of other human beings. These are impressive, carry significance for us and we remain fascinated by the stories of other people, particularly famous ones. So, what is different with the story of Jesus? Barth puts it like this:

> Here we have not to do with a reality different from God, nor with one of those earthly or even heavenly realities, but with God himself, with God in the highest, with the Creator of heaven and earth . . . This Jesus of Nazareth, who passes through the cities and villages of Galilee and wanders to Jerusalem, who is there accused and condemned and cruci-fied – this man is the Jehovah of the Old Testament, is the Creator, is God himself.[13]

The Jesus of Arius is a remarkable figure. He is the highest pin-nacle of creation, a wonderful example of what human life can be, someone to aspire to and imitate. He is 'the triumph of the human spirit'. Yet, in the last analysis, he does not tell us anything we could not see in any other remarkable human life. He might inspire us but he cannot reveal to us anything about ultimate reality, where we came from or anything definitive about what we are meant to become.

The Patristic debates about Christ have been accused of being overly rationalistic, a Platonizing of the gospel, with its language about substance, natures, being and so on. In the companion volume to this one, Katherine Sonderegger argues the contrary. It is precisely this kind of language, that speaks of fundamental ontology, that is appropriate because in Christ we are talking not just about a passing contingent historical figure but about the very deepest structure of reality.[14]

The assertion of the Nicene Creed that Jesus is 'of one being with the Father', made of the same stuff as the Father, as it were ('light from light, true God from true God'), tells us that, here, we are looking into the face of God our Creator, into the very heart of things. When we see Jesus reaching out to a woman accused of adultery, sending the crowd away with the realization that they have no right to stone her as they too are sinners no more or no less than she is – that is what God is like. When Jesus sees a crowd of thousands of people hungry for wisdom, but also for food, and he provides both – that is what God does. When Jesus dies on a cross, innocent yet condemned, and looks at his accusers and says, 'forgive them for they do not know what they are doing' – that is what God does. This is so much more than all those fine and inspiring pictures of what human beings can do. It is a picture of the very essence of reality. Here again, orthodoxy gives us a much bigger picture of the world, a richer and more hopeful vision of reality than we could find anywhere else. Here is a God who is, in very nature, generous, gracious kindness and love. As David Cohen, a former Director of Scripture Union once said: 'to limit yourself to the narrowness of God's revelation in Christ is to open yourself to the wide horizons of endless possibility.'

The Incarnation and meaning

However, there is more at stake here than information about God and the origins of the world. At stake is the very possibility of truth and meaning. George Steiner was one of the twentieth century's greatest literary critics and philosophers. In an insightful and luminous book entitled *Real Presences*, he raised the question of whether meaning is possible without a prior Word from God. He draws attention to the 'commentary on commentary' in modern life: the endless discussion, the academic industry of interpretations and reinterpretations that end up more confusing than clarifying with no closure on meaning and that ultimately militate against any final sense of truth. He argues that, unless we are addressed from the outside with a Word from God to which all our speech, art and activity is in some sense a response, our words simply float in mid-air with no reference to anything beyond themselves. For him, modernity has seen a crucial and seismic break from the confidence that our words refer to anything particular outside themselves: 'It is this break of the covenant between word and world which constitutes one of the very few genuine revolutions of spirit in Western history and which defines modernity itself.'[15] The literary project of deconstruction denies that there was in the beginning any Word at all, only the random play of sounds and markers in the mutations of time. He asks the perceptive question: 'can there be a secular poetics in the strict sense? Can there be an understanding of that which engenders "texts" and which makes their reception possible which is not underwritten by a postulate of transcendence?'[16]

He proposes a 'wager on transcendence', a 'presumption of presence'[17] yet, in the Incarnation, we find more than a wager: we find a promise. Robert Jenson argues that we are, at heart, storytelling people, yet we no longer have a world in which our stories make any sense.[18] We all have our different narratives, whether our own personal stories or the story of our community or ethnic group, which provide us with a sense of identity, yet this instinct rests on a deeper assumption that there is, ultimately, a true story about the universe and that each of our stories relate to and echo that true story to some degree or another. The Enlightenment project that sought a rational meaning without God was an attempt to retain a sense that there is meaning and a story that makes sense without a universal storyteller.

Perhaps the reason so many people in the modern world feel disconnected from each other, why loneliness and isolation are rampant, why there is a desperate search for identity, is because of this loss of an overarching story that tells us who we are within the world. If there is no Creator, we have to create ourselves. If there is no Word from God, our own words float free, devoid of any anchor to reality. If we live in a world where our stories increasingly compete with each other because there is no overarching story, we also live in a world where promises mean less because we have no sure sense of a future in which those promises can be kept. As Jenson puts it:

> either we will, however unknowingly, posit God, or we will lapse into nihilism . . . in which texts have no definite meaning . . . If there is no such God, then, at least for all we know . . . texts float free in a void of reference; should there be in fact something beyond language, it is out of our reach.[19]

The modern world is built on the idea of progress, yet all the Western secular ideas of progress are dim and faded echoes of the Christian narrative. The philosopher John Gray makes the point that secular progressive humanism is simply 'the Christian idea of history as a universal narrative of salvation dressed up in secular clothes'.[20] Western culture is built on the assumption of historical progress, which derives from the rejection of the cyclical nature of pagan views of the world and echoes instead the teleology of the Bible, which envisaged history moving towards the kingdom of God. For Gray, the problem with those modern myths of progress (whether the communist myth of a classless society, the capitalist myth of universal prosperity, the technological myth of transhumanism, or any other) is that they lack the Christian doctrine of sin, which always qualified human hubris that we were capable of building a great future for ourselves and the world.

The orthodoxy that we find articulated at Nicaea tells us that there is, after all, a Word from God, a Word that comes from outside our own contingent world, a primal Word to which all our words and actions are indeed a response and that enables us to discern whether our words are true and reliable or not. It also says that this Word is not a logical proposition but a person. At the same time, in the resurrection of Jesus Christ, in this assertion that 'on the third day he rose again according to the Scriptures', we are given a promise. We are given a picture of the future of humanity, the future of the world. The resurrected humanity of Jesus is a picture of the humanity into which we are intended to grow, each in our own particular way. It gives a promise that can be relied on because it is anchored in the resurrection itself.

Now of course, all this doesn't necessarily make it easy to discern whether or not our words or lives are true or false and whether they correspond to the Word spoken to us in Jesus Christ. It's not always easy to tell whether a particular social or ethical development or idea is in tune with the 'life of the world to come', as the creed puts. But it does give us a framework within which to do that thinking. And here again, we come to the idea that credal orthodoxy doesn't stop us thinking, in fact, it enables thinking. It gives us a framework of the nature of the world we live in – its origins, shape and destination within which to think in a way that makes sense. It gives us a world in which there is such a thing as sense and there are such things as truth and meaning, even if they need fine discernment to discover them.

In the previous chapter, we explored how the Christian understanding of creation out of nothing gives a metaphysics that grounds scientific exploration of the world. As we consider the way in which the Incarnation gives our own words the grounding in wider meaning and truth, it also becomes clear that the Incarnation is generative of new possibilities for art and the imagination.

We live in a world of images. We are surrounded by them every time we turn on a computer, read a magazine, or watch TV. Yet, as we flick through the latest video offerings online, we are reminded that these images are so often fleeting, insubstantial and mere distractions from the normal business of life. Reflecting on the generous orthodoxy of Nicaea, James K. A. Smith argues that the Incarnation, by asserting that flesh can do more than offer us a tentative picture of God, but can actually give us an encounter with God, gives a new depth and substance to art and representation. The belief that matter can be a conduit of grace opens up new possibilities for human imagination. As a result:

> the material can be at once fully physical and yet more; an artifact I see can also plumb the depths of the invisible, and can do so at both height and depth – slicing into the invisible corners of my own soul and the invisible heights of a cosmic Creator. Canvas, stone, string can become luminous because they can traffic in the mysterious.[21]

The generous incarnational orthodoxy of Nicaea, far from closing down thought and creativity, opens up new vistas for art and the imagination by offering us a world full of grace, a world where art can connect and represent something *out there*, rather than being obsessed with self-referential, angst-ridden reflection. Rather than dull, repetitive trivialized, forms of art that, having lost their metaphysical moorings, do little to inspire or energize, the faith of Nicaea gave birth to the huge pattern of church patronage of the arts and some of the greatest visual, verbal and architectural artistic forms the human race has ever produced.

Becoming like Jesus

As we have seen already, all that we have been thinking about – the Incarnation of the Son – is 'for us and for our salvation'. The Nicene

Creed does not just tell us that we can find knowledge of God in the face of Jesus Christ. It also tells of how God has broken into human life to make a real difference and tells us that this knowledge comes not just through intellectual enquiry but through spiritual growth.

Athanasius, reflecting on the wording of the Creed of Nicaea in his *De Incarnatione*, makes the fundamental point that the Incarnation is about the renewal of creation. It is true that Jesus Christ gives us true knowledge of God yet it is also clear that this is not objective, abstract, intellectual understanding. The Word became flesh not just because we did not know God but because we are far from him, and our very humanity slowly dissolves as we move away from the source of life, which is God himself. For Athanasius, sinful acts do not just contravene divine law, they eat away at our souls like spiritual bacteria in a form of inner corruption that will ultimately destroy us. Therefore, to rescue us, God has entered into the very heart of human life, renewing it from within. Those who are in Christ therefore participate in the renewal of all things, beginning with the renewal of human nature itself. His death is the overcoming of death and the resurrection is the reversal of the process of corruption.

For Athanasius, this Christology is no mere abstract intellectual game. Our very survival, or our salvation, is at stake. The Incarnation is nothing less than a matter of life and death. The Creed of Nicaea is an invitation not just to believe in these articles of faith but to live as if they are true, to stake our lives on it. Belief, life, death, decay and revival are all bound up together here. Towards the conclusion of this work, Athanasius writes:

> For the searching and right understanding of the Scriptures there is need of a good life and a pure soul, and for Christian virtue to guide the mind to grasp, so far as human nature can, the truth concerning God the Word. One cannot possibly understand the teaching of the saints unless one has a pure mind and is trying to imitate their life.[22]

Athanasius, like Augustine and most other Patristic writers, sees this process of wrestling to say the right thing about God, of seeking to understand the dynamics of the relationship between the Father and the Son, not purely as an academic task but as one that requires spiritual and devotional involvement.

Much recent scholarship on Nicaea, its origins, and its legacy emphasizes that we cannot understand these debates outside the context of the need to grow in knowledge of God and in holiness and virtue. In resisting the ideas of Arius, Nicaea had insisted on the possibility of created beings sharing in the very life of God by sharing in Christ who himself shares the divine nature. Rowan Williams points to the later spirituality of Gregory of Nyssa or Augustine as fruit of this and what he calls 'a steady and endless enlarging of the heart through union in prayer and virtue with the Word, which is also a steady and endless growth in knowledge of the Father'.[23]

In a related way, Lewis Ayres shows how the pro-Nicene theologians of the later fourth century focused on paying attention to the distinction between Creator and creation, and the divine economy (the way in which God acts towards us), but did all this 'only to draw us slowly towards a contemplation of the divine realities of which they speak.'[24] For them, salvation happens through participation in Christ where the purified soul reflects the Word with whom it has become united. Sin is a problem not so much because it renders us guilty before God and in need of forgiveness but because it confuses and distorts our spiritual vision. It distorts the focus of the soul on God and inhibits our ability to pay proper attention to God. For these thinkers, the core of theological practise should be the contemplation of Scripture, which enables the contemplation of the mystery of God revealed in Jesus Christ.

The Arian tendency to draw a hard line between the unknowable oneness of God and all created things made knowledge of and participation in God a logical and spiritual impossibility. We could grow in imitation of him but not sharing in his life. Nicene faith, by contrast, expands the possibilities for human life, inviting us into a Holy Communion with God in Jesus Christ and the possibility of real, profound transformation of mind, soul and, ultimately in the resurrection, even of our bodies.

This is the Son of God becoming human, not *a* human, and changing the very nature of humanity by that very act. This shifts the ground under the feet of every human being whether we recognize it or not. It tells us who we are: relational beings who need help, who need God and other people to be our true selves. It tells us who God is: full of grace and truth. It gives us grounds for believing our words can correspond to reality. It invites us into a growing intimacy with our Creator to expand our hearts and our vision. It tells us that, in Jesus Christ, we do not see just another fine picture of human capacity to inspire us to emulation or perhaps to depress us at how far short we fall of our own potential. Instead, we see God himself reaching out to us in our weakness, compromise and failure, and enabling our hearts to grow in their capacity to love the God who loves us and all those made in his image. He gives us not just a passing gift, but he gives us himself.

This is a truly generous orthodoxy, yet it remains to be seen how it faces up to human rejection of grace, a theme the next chapter picks up.

4

Dead and buried

At this point, something remarkable happens in the creed. Having spelled out the extraordinary idea that the God who created the universe has become one of us – eating, laughing, sleeping, sorrowing, the playwright stepping on to the stage of his own play – it then reminds us that we killed him.

The story is so familiar to us that we so often fail to grasp its enormity. The lines we have just been exploring in the creed take us high, very high. We are given this dizzying vision of the exalted Christ, the only Son of the Father, the Eternal One begotten before all time now in human flesh, the One through whom and for whom everything exists, the One whose character is found in every living thing. It then plunges as low as you can possibly imagine in saying that the eternal Word, the one beloved of the Father, was *crucified* under Pontius Pilate.

The more the early Christians reflected on this, the greater the scandal appeared, especially as the Church became more respectable after its adoption by Emperor Constantine in the early fourth century. When the creed of 325 was edited at Constantinople in 381, the simple word 'he suffered' (*pathónta*) was expanded into 'He was crucified for us under Pontius Pilate, and suffered, and was buried', as if they wanted to emphasize the shame of it, his deadness and the apparent finality of this event.

This death took place in a particular time and a particular place. Jesus' blood dripped on to real dust. The cross marked out for him was rooted in Palestinian rock, lodged in a crevice in a stony outcrop in a disused quarry just outside the walls of first-century Jewish Jerusalem during the procuratorship of Pontius Pilate, an otherwise undistinguished and forgettable civil servant in a relatively obscure part of the Roman Empire.

The manner of death could not take us lower either. Crucifixion, as is well known, was excruciating, a death reserved for enemies of the empire – runaway slaves, violent criminals, rebellious foreigners and rebels. It was also a deliberately public event. The message was simple: mess with the empire and this is what will happen to you.

Other work has been done on the social and cultural meaning of crucifixion.[1] Yet our focus here is what those early Christians chose to say about this seminal event in their brief, stripped down description: what it says about God, what it says about us, how it relates to a generous orthodoxy and how it gives us a map for our journey through the complexities of life.

The anthropological deficit

The Nicene Creed doesn't have a separate section on human nature. Its focus is pointedly and deliberately on the nature of God. It is primarily theological not anthropological. Yet the creed does tell us two things about ourselves: that we are created by God and that we need help. Christ came into the world 'for us and for our salvation'. It is unflattering, but it tells us that we need saving.

The creed even repeats it: 'he was crucified *for us*'. Creeds are deliberately brief. They don't waste words. When there are only 175 words in the Greek text of the creed, to repeat something means that it matters. This whole story of Incarnation, crucifixion and resurrection was *for us*. At the very least, the thing we need saving from is the guilt that lies over us as a human race: that when our maker came to us, we tried to kill him.

The story says that we are all involved in this. Within the worldview of the authors of the New Testament, one of the most fundamental divisions was between Jew and Gentile. The story makes clear that both played a part in the death of Jesus. Although Gentile Christians have been tempted over the years to blame the Jews, it is explicitly clear in the Gospel accounts that both the

Jewish hierarchy and the Roman imperial regime were responsible. If anything, the creed reminds us Gentiles that we bear the burden of guilt by the mention of Pontius Pilate rather than Caiaphas the High Priest. Though it barely crosses our minds most of the time, within the framework that the creed gives us, the whole of the human race stands guilty of this crime of attempting to kill God.

This was the great sin. All our other petty sins are dim echoes of this one. Thoughtless greed that denies the poor food or shelter; our crushing, lingering words to a friend or spouse; envy of those who succeed where we don't; lust that treats another person as a means of satisfying our own desire and dispenses of them when we are sated, all of these bear the telltale mark of rejection of God and his generosity. As Karl Barth puts it (in his 1940s gender-specific language):

> Sin means to reject the grace of God . . . For the first time we are faced here with the root of all great and petty transgressions . . . Where we are guilty towards man, we are automatically reminded of *this* man. For every man whom we have offended and tormented is one of those whom Jesus Christ has called his brethren.[2]

Yet it is not only sins against our fellow humans of which we are guilty. Perhaps the greatest sin that incriminates us all right now is our slow choking of the planet we were given to care for. We are all implicated. Every time I use a plastic bag, eat chocolate, drink coffee or cow's milk, drive my car or fly in a plane I am caught up in the complex network of causes that is driving climate change and global injustice. In our globally networked world, where products reach us through a bewildering chain of producers and transit arrangements, it is almost inevitable that, somewhere along the line, someone will have been unfairly treated and the environment damaged to enable us to consume and enjoy the things we assume are our right. It is virtually impossible to live in our intricately networked world without some involvement in its injustices. We killed God and now we are killing his world. In the terms of Nicene orthodoxy, the killing of Jesus was a rejection of his divine identity, and our destruction of the planet is a similar rejection of the creation that is an expression of the divine love between Father, Son and Spirit.

With all this in mind, lament becomes the only appropriate stance and, in some of the most perceptive works of art and culture, is only too readily apparent. A short post-apocalyptic film entitled *All of This Unreal Time* appeared in 2021, in the middle of the second year of the COVID pandemic, featuring the actor Cillian Murphy lamenting and confessing pretty much everything – guilt towards other people, the cost of unsustainable lifestyles, the shame of mistakes and missed opportunities. In a monologue confession, spoken to no one in particular and maybe even to an absent God, he begins:

> I came out here to apologize. I find myself, at the midpoint of my life, in a dark wood, and now I'm here, in the forest of my mind, and every tree is shame, every living thing is a reprimand, and I realize, I must speak freely now, before I lose you.[3]

The film takes place mainly in grimy urban landscapes with a dark feel of sober regret, yet it captures something haunting and real, more real than the shallow glitz of celebrity culture or the endless stream of narcissistic social media self-promotion. It breathes lament – a sense of sadness for the human condition, a sorrow for our original sin, capturing the deeply ingrained generational nature of sin: 'it's cultures deep, it's Dad's fault – back and back and back',[4] even perhaps back to an apple eaten from a tree, or our execution of the author of life – yet, at the same time, it realizes that even the deep historical roots of sin don't allow us to escape our personal responsibility for it.

The death of God

St Paul spoke of Christ crucified as 'the power of God and the wisdom of God' (1 Cor. 1.24). It was Tertullian that first used rhetorical language of 'God dying' and a 'crucified God' and modern theologians such as Jürgen Moltmann have taken up the theme.[5] However, theologians of the Patristic period generally denied the idea of the suffering of God. In particular, they identified the 'Patripassian' heresy, rejecting the idea that the Father suffers in the suffering of the Son on the cross. In short, if God is eternal and suffering is taken into the very heart of God, then suffering itself becomes eternal and we have no hope that it will ever be finally banished as the Christian faith has always maintained it will be. Also, it is unclear how a God who is enveloped by suffering rather than resisting it can rescue us from it. In saying that the Son of God suffered on the cross, the general idea of the early Fathers was that his capacity to experience suffering derived from his human nature, yet his divine nature worked in and through his humanity to resist, endure and overcome suffering, not being overcome by it in the way that we are.[6]

In more modern times, the theme of the death of God was most famously taken up by Friedrich Nietzsche. In an often-quoted scene from *The Gay Science,* he imagines a madman lighting a lantern on a sunny day and rushing into the marketplace, shouting that he is searching for God. It's worth quoting the scene at some length. To the mocking bemusement of his hearers, he responds:

We have killed him – you and I. All of us are his murderers. But how did we do this? How could we drink up the sea? Who gave us the sponge to wipe away the entire horizon? What were we doing when we unchained this earth from its sun? Whither is it moving now? Whither are we moving? Away from all suns? Are we not plunging continually? Backward, sideward, forward, in all directions? Is there still any up or down? Are we not straying, as through an infinite nothing? Do we not feel the breath of empty space? Has it not become colder? Is not night continually closing in on us? Do we not need to light lanterns in the morning? Do we hear nothing as yet of the noise of the gravediggers who are burying God? Do we smell nothing as yet of the divine decomposition? Gods, too, decompose. God is dead. God remains dead. And we have killed him.

How shall we comfort ourselves, the murderers of all murderers? What was holiest and mightiest of all that the world has yet owned has bled to death under our knives: who will wipe this blood off us? What water is there for us to clean ourselves? What festivals of atonement, what sacred games shall we have to invent? Is not the greatness of this deed too great for us? Must we ourselves not become gods simply to appear worthy of it? There has never been a greater deed; and whoever is born after us – for the sake of this deed he will belong to a higher history than all history hitherto.[7]

Reading this while standing beside the cross with the Son of God dying before our very eyes is striking. Nietzsche's madman (who is, of course, saner than any of us) sees clearly the implications of the death of God in the Western world's gradual rejection of him. There is the sense of guilt ('what were we doing?' 'Do we not feel the breath of empty space?'), there is the need for some kind of expiation ('who will wipe this blood off us?'), and he goes on to remark that the implications of this seismic event have yet to be realized ('I have come too early . . . my time is not yet . . . it has not yet reached the ears of men').

Nietzsche's own answer to these questions is that God needs to die to allow a new type of human to emerge. He laments the Christian values of pity and humility that have 'made the great virtuous ones, of whom antiquity had no lack, vanish forever from the earth, those popular men, who in their belief in their perfection, walked about with the dignity of a hero of the bull-fight'.[8] Only if God is dead can this new humanity – what he calls the *Übermensch* or Superman – appear. Although, as we look back on the Nazi glorification of the brave Aryan Teutonic hero with which Nietzsche's vision became inextricably linked, we may be less sure that this was a good idea.

Terry Eagleton calls Nietzsche 'the first real atheist'. He continues: 'of course there had been unbelievers in abundance before him, but it is Nietzsche above all who confronts the terrifying, exhilarating consequences of the death of God.[9] Since the Enlightenment, all kinds of other ideas and ideals have taken the place of God as the supreme value, something worth living and dying for – reason, freedom, art, culture, the nation state, the revolution, and so on. Yet, as the philosopher and cultural critic John Gray argues, the Enlightenment project has just been a failed attempt to replace God with other ideals so that communism, fascism and liberal humanism, for example, are just different secular versions of Christian eschatology: hoping for a bright future kingdom to come one day, just replacing trust in God with a trust in politics or human goodness and ingenuity to bring it about, yet without the dose of realism that the Christian doctrine of the Fall retains.

For Gray, the Enlightenment was an attempt at 're-founding morality and society on universal, tradition-independent rational principles',[10] yet it was always doomed to failure. He argues that we need to relinquish any search for grounds for universal truth or morality, instead making the best of the postmodern condition of fractured perspectives and groundless practises. At the same time, he finds postmodernism itself, with its attempt at self-creation through deconstruction, shallow and incoherent and advocates instead for abandoning any idea of a universal world culture and denying an anthropocentric view of the world. Nietzsche punctures the bubble of the Enlightenment world, showing that, if God is dead, there can no longer be any universal grounds for truth, reason and morality. In the words of the Christian theologian John Hughes: 'Nietzsche can help us see that if people are going to be consistent in abandoning God, then perhaps they should abandon belief in truth and goodness as we have known them as well.'[11]

Nietzsche recognizes that you can kill God but, if you do, you kill any sense of meaning as well. If we imagine there is some broad sense to things, it follows to ask where it comes from. Terry Eagleton puts it graphically:

Having murdered the Creator in the most spectacular of all Oedipal revolts, we have hidden the body, repressed all memory of the traumatic event, tidied up the scene of the crime and behave as though we are innocent of the act . . . modern secular societies have effectively disposed of God but find it morally and politically convenient, even imperative, to behave as though they have not.[12]

We still act as if life means something, that human beings are valuable, that the earth is worth protecting even though, as we have seen in George Steiner, John Gray and others, we have few grounds for claiming these things. We are living off the fumes of the Christian revelation. There is a connection between our rejection of God in recent centuries and our rejection of his Son when he came among us. The former is just an echo of the latter, a gloomy repetition of the fatal human tendency to try to live without limits, to think we can create ourselves, to spurn the joy set before us, to refuse the grace that permeates this world. There is also a connection between these things and the loss of an overarching framework that makes sense of life, history and also our petty sins, those small-scale snubs to a God who comes before us in the shape of other people – his image-bearers – who cross our path each day. Lament and confession are the only appropriate response to the darkness in the human heart that makes us turn away from our Creator and turn away from each other.

He suffered death and was buried

At this point of the creed, all hope seems lost. The Son of God is dead and buried. Yet there is that 'for our sake'. Hidden behind the darkness, God is still there, although imperceptible even by Jesus as he utters his cry of abandonment by God. All this happened 'for us and for our salvation'. The crucifixion may be our darkest hour, but it is also the moment at which the first glimmers of the dawn begin to appear.

When it comes to soteriology, or the doctrine of salvation, the creeds are relatively restrained. They do not tend to lay down any particular doctrine of the atonement. The Nicene Creed leaves a fair degree of latitude and space for debate and discussion about different understandings of exactly how Christ's Incarnation and sufferings effect redemption, but simply states that it was precisely 'for our salvation' that all this happened.[13]

It is perhaps another example of the way in which the creeds invite rather than close down thought, opening out a generous intellectual and theological space rather than limiting it. By this bald and bold statement, it sets the soteriological parameters – that, despite its appearance and even the intent of its perpetrators, the cross was not a meaningless event. As the culmination of the sufferings of Christ throughout his life with us, it has saved us. On the cross, the God who made the world, in the form of the Son, enters into the most intense form of suffering, which is not only physical but mental and spiritual. He visits the place of utter abandonment where even God himself appears to have deserted him. He storms the fortress of evil by entering its dark heart and overcoming it once and for all. Words begin to fail us when we describe this momentous event, which resonates inside all our stories of trial, the triumph of good over evil, of redemptive suffering.

The creed, in its minimal description of this, invites us to explore ways in which we can make sense of this remarkable announcement, sending us back to the Scriptures to explore what they say and to discern ways to speak of this mystery, although perhaps warning us not to fall out over different readings of this simple yet world-changing claim – that, as St Paul had said, 'Christ died for our sins in accordance with the Scriptures' (1 Cor. 15.3). Again, Barth gets it right: 'Do not confuse my theory of the reconciliation with the thing itself. All theories of reconciliation can be but pointers. But do you also pay attention to this "for us."'[14]

One particular benefit the creed does highlight is that baptism, which inscribes the pattern of death and resurrection in the life of a particular person, is 'for the forgiveness of sins'. We live in a culture that finds forgiveness very difficult. When someone has transgressed particular social rules, whether of right or left, in the past or the present, they are quickly cancelled with no apparent means of redemption. Tweets are dredged up from the past, passing comments are reinterpreted and mistakes are highlighted in a way that enables the critic to take the moral high ground and the original sinner to be silenced. None of us can claim that we have never said or done anything of which we're ashamed – we just hope it doesn't come to light. We are perhaps living in the most puritan and unforgiving times that we can remember and the cross and resurrection of Jesus speaks powerfully of the possibility of forgiveness and redemption from past sins and mistakes.

What comes next widens our eyes even more:

On the third day he rose again
in accordance with the Scriptures;
he ascended into heaven
and is seated at the right hand of the Father.
He will come again in glory to judge the living and the dead,
and his kingdom will have no end.

This is why Dorothy Sayers called the story of Christian orthodoxy 'the most exciting drama that has ever staggered the imagination of man'.[15] This is no bland narrative weaving its way through the grey compromises and small-scale nuances of our ordinary existence. It goes from the highest to the lowest place then back again to the most exalted place of all – the sight of Jesus stirring from the slab on which his body was laid, rolling back the stone, startling those early risers on the first day of the new world and ascending to the throne of the universe with the promise that he will one day rule an everlasting kingdom.

If Jesus remains dead, that is the end of Christianity. If he has been raised, it is the beginning of a new world. The resurrection is either a historical curiosity, a fossil from the past, or the cornerstone of a new way of looking at and living in the world. The Gnostics, always in the back of the Patristic mind, were only ever interested in a resurrection of the soul. After all, salvation was not through the sacrifice of Christ but instead through knowledge imparted to the elect. Even Origen didn't quite get this, believing that the resurrection was symbolic of a spiritual resurrection, leaving behind the flesh.

Tertullian, in taking on the Gnostics, refused that option and argued that bodies matter. What we do with them matters – sex matters, politics matter, creation matters and suffering is real. His image is of bodies renewed not replaced, like battered ships putting into a harbour with torn sails and cracked masts, yet not sold to the scrapyard but refitted and restored for a new journey. That is why the resurrection of the *body* mattered to him.

The resurrection of Jesus meant the defeat of the enemies of humankind: sin, the devil and death itself. Athanasius drew the implication that, if death was overcome, there was no more room for fear of anything as our greatest fear is the fear of death. This where the power of the martyrs came from: that not even those who kill them can overcome them:

All the disciples of Christ despise death; they take the offensive against it and, instead of fearing it, by the sign of the cross and by faith in Christ trample on it as on something dead. Before the divine sojourn of the Saviour, even the holiest of men were afraid of death, and mourned the dead as those who perish. But now that the Saviour has raised His body, death is no longer terrible, but all those who believe in Christ tread it underfoot as nothing, and prefer to die rather than to deny their faith in Christ, knowing full well that when they die they do not perish, but live indeed, and become incorruptible through the resurrection.[16]

This is where Christian orthodoxy cuts across the anxious, fearful snatching for pleasure in the ancient and modern worlds. One of Horace's Odes runs like this:

Strain your wine and prove your wisdom; life is short;
   should hope be more?
In the moment of our talking, envious time has ebbed away.
Seize the present; trust tomorrow e'en as little as you may.[17]

Carpe Diem: seize the day. It is the essence of the Epicurean view of the world and Western societies are full of materialist Epicurean sentiment. The film *Dead Poets Society* claimed the phrase in its hymn to modern expressive individualism. Life is fleeting and it won't last long so make your life extraordinary and grab what pleasure you can while you can. If this world is all there is, if death is simply the dissolving of atoms into the earth, if the only hope of afterlife is in some thin idea of the circle of life where our decaying remains provide the manure out of which future plants and flowers grow, then Epicurean ethics is really the only option. Hence the desperate search for exhilarating experiences – bucket lists, trading in a marriage partner for a better model if they cease to satisfy, acquiring the resources we need to fulfil our dream – because, if this world is all we have, our dreams can only be realized in this world.

Yet, if resurrection happened, if Jesus is not a dead poet but the firstfruits of the new heavens and new earth, the first crocus of spring heralding many more to come, then this world is not all there is and the frantic urgency to 'seize the day' begins to fade away. It becomes okay *not* to grasp everything, but to be content with simple things like food and clothing (1 Tim. 6.8). Fear of missing out is not the worst thing after all. Sticking with difficult situations and difficult people even until the end of life becomes possible. Babies born with disabilities, adults with mental illnesses, the elderly with dementia are not lesser forms of life because they are unable to 'seize the day' like the young and gifted. Not getting everything you want here and now is fine because we were never meant to anyway. This island may have its delights, but we can't taste them all and, in any case, the point is to find our way to that narrow isthmus that leads to a great land beyond.

Nietzsche and Nicaea

Nietzsche had a powerful insight into the implications of the death of God yet he never seemed to grasp the relevance of Easter. Likewise, John Gray looks out with a degree of sober pessimism on a world where it is impossible either to revive the Enlightenment dream of a secular eschatology or to rebuild a premodern, enchanted Christian world. The Enlightenment imagined the individual moral agent, now properly enlightened and freed from the restraint of tradition, hierarchy and divine purpose, as sovereign and free in his or her own moral authority. Yet it still wanted to cling on to some kind of moral framework even though any idea of teleology or purpose was taken away. We ended up with simple emotivism or subjectivism where moral authority can only come from within our own souls and desires rather than from any external source, and moral judgements are really about preferences rather than aligning with any wider moral structure of the world. Therefore, in Gray's words, 'we no longer possess anything like a coherent moral vocabulary, any specification of the human good or of the virtues in terms of which moral reasoning can proceed'.[18] We no longer believe the metaphysics of the Christian view of the world, yet still want its moral structure and some kind of hope for the future. But it's far from clear where those are going to come from. Gray argues for a kind of 'letting things be' rather than subjecting them to our human purposes. He imagines a new, more passive relationship with our natural environment where we are less in control and less keen to dominate and subdue the earth.

Yet he does not envisage the significance of resurrection, and neither does he take into account the fullness of the Christian vision of humanity at the heart of creation. He bewails the influence of the Christian idea – that humans are made in the image of God and therefore uniquely special – as part of the cause of our problems, leading to precisely the kind of ecological domination and despoilment that we see all around us. Yet he never seems to take on board the equally important idea in the book of Genesis that bearing the divine image involves a particular responsibility to care for and protect the rest of creation, a new vocation for humanity that the old Adam has dismally failed to discharge.

The new Adam, Jesus, is different. According to the Nicene Creed, it is the very Son of God through whom all things were made who has been crucified and risen and ascended to the right hand of the Father as the judge of all. This brings an invitation for human beings to be remade in his image, the image of the second Adam, instead of being conformed to what the first Adam has become.

Reflecting on Nietzsche's idea of God's demise, leading to the emergence of the *Übermensch*, Terry Eagleton points out the irony:

> That the death of God involves the death of Man, along with the birth of a new form of humanity, is orthodox Christian doctrine, a fact of which Nietzsche seems not to have been aware. The incarnation is the place where both God and Man undergo a kind of kenosis or self-humbling symbolised by the self-dispossession of Christ. Only through this tragic self-emptying can a new humanity hope to emerge. In its solidarity with the outcast and afflicted the crucifixion is a critique of all hubristic humanism.[19]

Both Nietzsche and Nicaea see the death of God leading to the death and rebirth of humanity. Both see the death of God (though they locate that event differently) as the turning point of history. For Nietzsche, the death of God leads to the birth of the *Übermensch*. For Nicaea, the death of God leads to the resurrection of Christ and the rebirth of the human race, yet it looks very different from Nietzsche's vision.

Nietzsche foresees the death of God as leading to the death of meaning, truth and humanity as we have known it. Yet there is another sense in which the death of God leads to a human death – yours and mine. In the Gospels, Jesus, predicting his own death, says, 'If any want to become my followers, let them deny themselves and take up their cross and follow me. For those who want to save their life will lose it, and those who lose their life for my sake will find it' (Matt. 16.24–25).

Similarly, 1 Peter 2.24 reads, 'He himself bore our sins in his body on the cross', yet the implication drawn is not that we might immediately live the resurrection life, but 'so that we might *die* to sins and live for righteousness' (1 Peter 2.24 NIV). The pattern of death and resurrection is the only way in which the new humanity comes to birth in us. It is foreshadowed through the descent into death and rising to new life of baptism and then enacted, putting to death destructive and damaging desires here and now, in anticipation of resurrection in the future.

Christ died not only that we might live but that we also might die. The pathway to life passes through self-denial, taking up the shameful cross. Notice how different this is. We live in a world where we have convinced ourselves that the route to happiness, in fact the only way to live, is self-fulfilment, the gratification of desire and the absolute value of personal choice. We live through the narcissistic self-celebration of social media, believing that we deserve to be entertained, are entitled to comfort and the freedom to engage in the pursuit of happiness as we want to, where the fulfilled life has to consist of getting what we want on our own terms. We give to others and change the world only as long as it doesn't inconvenience us too much. We have decided that self-denial is oppression and self-fulfilment is the only way to true happiness.

This is another of those places where the map of life given to us by the creeds offers a very different picture of the landscape, an alternative route through the island that leads to the narrow isthmus that leads to the great land beyond. For many Christians, this death has been literal, yet for all Christians there is a kind of death.

The way of life implied by the story of the creeds involves a 'no' as well as a 'yes', just as they offer us a map for the journey that, at the same time, closes off a number of what seem like promising routes. Learning to love my neighbour necessarily requires saying 'no' to things I would love to do. Living within the boundaries of my created bodily limitations, and resisting the temptations that pull at me and that long for fulfilment will be hard. Learning to give away and let go of things that I possess but do not need does not come easy. Siding with and living alongside those whose path of life is difficult and who are not among the influencers, whether the economically poor, the victims of injustice – in other words, those like Jesus – means I cannot fulfil my every wish and desire. But then if 'he rose again in accordance with the Scriptures; ascended into heaven and is seated at the right hand of the Father, and will come again in glory to judge the living and the dead, and his kingdom will have no end', then maybe that's not to be feared after all.

John Gray may be right that there is no return to a simple premodern Christian world. Nostalgia is not the answer. So, the task of the Church is not to try to rebuild that world of Christendom but to do as the early Christians did – bear witness to the resurrection and the promise of a new world. Irenaeus and Tertullian had no idea that the opportunity to build a Christian civilization was around the corner but, whether it came or not and whatever form it took, their task was to keep reminding the world that Jesus has risen from the dead. What happens as a result of that witness – whether the church remains a voice crying in the wilderness or a new form of society emerges that reflects the values of the kingdom of God – that is above our pay grade and in the hands of God. Our simple task is to keep bearing witness.

Yet we are not alone in this. This pathway through the island of life, bearing witness to anyone who will listen to the resurrection of Jesus and the coming resurrection of all that is found in him, the path of becoming someone formed by generosity, is not one of strenuous moral effort. It is one where a power is at work in us and within the world to shape us not into the *Übermensch* – that vision of power, independence and force – but into the generosity, humility and compassion of a new kind of human being – the new humanity in Christ.

5

The giver of life

Reflecting on the development of Christian doctrine, Gregory of Nazianzus, one of the giants of fourth-century Christian theology, once wrote this:

> The old covenant made clear proclamation of the Father, a less definite one of the Son. The new covenant made the Son manifest and gave us a glimpse of the Spirit's Godhead. At the present time, the Spirit resides amongst us, giving us a clearer manifestation of himself than before. It was dangerous for the Son to be preached openly when the Godhead of the Father was still unacknowledged. It was dangerous, too, for the Holy Spirit to be made . . . an extra burden when the Son had not been received. It could mean men jeopardizing what did lie within their powers, as happens to those encumbered with a diet too strong for them, or who gaze at sunlight with eyes as yet too feeble for it. No, God meant it to be by piecemeal additions . . . by progress and advance from glory to glory, that the light of the Trinity should shine upon more illustrious souls.[1]

Gregory reveals the gradual process by which the doctrine of the Trinity emerged in the first centuries of the Church and he attributes a level of providence to it. For him, full Trinitarian orthodoxy is strong meat that needs a healthy stomach, a dazzling bright light that can only be seen by those accustomed to looking at lesser light. So, the doctrine of the full divinity of the Spirit could only be addressed after the issue of the divine nature of the Son was resolved, as it were. This chapter explores the arguments that

surrounded the creeds' affirmations on the Spirit and their implications for the map of reality that this generous credal orthodoxy
gives.

Nicaea and the Spirit

After its lengthy clause on the theology of the Son, the Council of
Nicaea in 325 included just one single line for its third article. It
wasn't even a line, just a sub-clause: 'and in the Holy Spirit'.

This obviously left a huge number of questions unanswered.
Who or what was the Holy Spirit? Was it divine or created? What
did it do? Was it a person or an impersonal force? Over the course
of the fourth century, a vigorous debate ensued about the status
of the Holy Spirit and its relationship to the Father and the Son,
particularly involving the Cappadocian Fathers – Basil the Great,
his brother, Gregory of Nyssa, and his great friend, Gregory of
Nazianzus – all in opposition to figures such as the deposed Bishop
of Constantinople, Macedonius. Summing up the results of this
debate, the Council of Constantinople in 381 AD expanded this
simple line into the much more familiar clause on the Holy Spirit
that we know from the Nicene Creed said in many churches to this
day.

The Creed of 381 makes two main changes to the earlier version
of the Nicene Creed. The original creed of 325 simply described
how the Son

for us men and for our salvation came down,
and became incarnate, and was made man

The Creed of 381 amended this to:

For us men and for our salvation
he came down from heaven:
by the power of the Holy Spirit
he became incarnate from the Virgin Mary, and was made
    man

It then went on to expand the simple sub-clause on the Holy Spirit to read this:

> We believe in the Holy Spirit, the Lord, the giver of Life,
> who proceeds from the Father.
> With the Father and the Son he is worshipped and glorified.
> He has spoken through the Prophets.

Nicene orthodoxy therefore asserts four things about the Holy Spirit: that it was by the Spirit that the Incarnation took place; that the Spirit is the giver of life; that the Spirit is worshipped alongside and with the Father and the Son, and that it is the Spirit who speaks through the words of prophets and preachers.

All of this reflects these fourth-century debates about the Spirit, just as the Creed of 325 reflected third-century debates on Christology. So, in our exploration of the nature of a generous credal orthodoxy, it is worth looking back at those debates to see some of the trajectories of thought that led to these changes and some of their implications for our understanding of a generous orthodoxy, its ability to generate creative thought and action and to form our lives today.

The Spirit and divine life

The creed as finalized at Constantinople in 381 asserted that it was by the Spirit that Christ was born of the Virgin Mary. In other words, the Incarnation was a fully Trinitarian event, with the Father sending the Spirit upon Mary to enable her to give birth to God the Son. This is a paradigm for all the works of God in that everything God does involves Father, Son and Holy Spirit. We have already seen how the Father creates through the Son and perfects through the Spirit, yet these are not three separate tasks but one work of creation. In the same way, the Incarnation is one indivisible act of God, whereby he acts to rescue human life. As Athanasius put it: 'The Father does all things through the Word and in the Holy Spirit.'[2] In both creation and the Incarnation, God shapes and forms what he has created by the Holy Spirit.

So, the Spirit perfects us in divine holiness in a particular way. St Paul writes of how the Spirit alone enables us to pray. It is by the Spirit that we find the instinct growing within us to call out to God as our Father. Now again, as we saw in the description of God as the 'Father Almighty' in the first article of the creed, the Father is first and foremost the Father of Jesus before he is our Father. St Paul captures this by saying, 'You have received a Spirit of adoption. When we cry, "Abba! Father!" it is that very Spirit bearing witness with our spirit that we are children of God' (Rom. 8.15–16), or 'God has sent the Spirit of his Son into our hearts, crying, "Abba! Father!" So you are no longer a slave but a child' (Gal. 4.6–7).

Of course, 'Abba' is the intimate word of address that Jesus alone uses for God (Mark 14.36). Paul's insight is that the Spirit draws us into the same relationship with the Father as Jesus himself enjoys, although not separately from Christ, as if we had some direct access to God as co-equal sons and daughters alongside him, but by being united with Christ, so that in him, we share his intimacy with the Father. As Basil put it: 'Through the Spirit we become intimate with God.'[3] The image he uses is that of adoption. Christ is the natural Son, we are sons and daughters by adoption yet treated the same as the Son and entitled to use the same language in addressing the Father as Jesus, the natural Son.

The relationship between Father and Son is one of pure, simple love. At Jesus' baptism, the voice from the Father declares 'this is my Son whom I love'. John's Gospel tells us that 'the Father loves the Son' (John 3.35, 5.20). So, we might say that the way in which the Spirit matures us is by drawing us ever deeper into the love between the Father and the Son, the love at the heart of God out of which the world came into being. St Augustine often called the Spirit the 'bond of love' between the Father and the Son.[4] So, the deeper we are drawn into the life of the Spirit, the deeper we find ourselves enveloped by this love between Father and Son. Yet this is no static, impersonal, object but an active, searching love that longs to bring the rest of creation into that embrace. In fact, the Spirit brings creation to its fulfilment precisely in this way, by drawing it more and more deeply into the love that pulses at the heart of God between the Father and the Son.[5]

As this happens, we begin to find the world opening out anew before us, starting with our approach to the created order around us.

The Spirit and creation

The creed calls the Spirit the 'giver of life'. The second verse of the Bible speaks of the Spirit of God who 'swept over the face of the waters' (Gen. 1.2). This idea of the Spirit's involvement in creation was picked up by the Cappadocians. Gregory of Nyssa wrote:

> The Spirit is everywhere and present to each thing, filling the earth and remaining in the heavens, poured out among the super-terrestrial powers, filling all things according to the worth of each, and yet losing nothing of his own fullness.[6]

The Spirit gives life to all things and yet there is a specific role that the Spirit plays in creation that is brought out in particular by Gregory's own brother, Basil the Great.

Back in the second century, Irenaeus had already identified the particular work of the Spirit, which was to bring creation to maturity, to its fulfilment:

> What could the visible fruit of the invisible Spirit be, if not to make flesh mature and receptive of imperishability . . . The Holy Spirit is sent to the entire universe, and since creation, has been transforming it, carrying it towards the final resurrection.[7]

Basil picks up this idea and develops it in his work *On the Holy Spirit*, which appeared around 375 AD and which influenced the new clauses that ended up in the Nicene Creed in 381. For him, angels 'exist by the will of the Father, are brought into being by the work of the Son, and are perfected by the presence of the Spirit . . . The Originator of all things is One: He creates through the Son and perfects through the Spirit.'[8]

In a previous chapter, we looked at Basil's fascination with the natural world in his sermons on the creation story in Genesis. As he contemplates the creation, he comments that, just as the sun nourishes the physical life of plants, created things that seek to grow into their proper fullness need to be turned towards the Spirit: 'He waters them with his life-giving breath and helps them reach their proper fulfilment. He perfects all other things, and himself lacks nothing . . . Through him . . . those who progress are brought to perfection.'[9] The Spirit directs us to the 'life of the world to come' as the Nicene Creed was to put it.

It is not for nothing that the Spirit is called the *Holy* Spirit. The primary work of the Spirit is to make things holy or, to put it in ways we might be more familiar with, to enable them to become their true selves, to become what they were made to be. Elsewhere, Basil makes a distinction between our being made in the image and the likeness of God. Every human being is made in the image of God, yet has the opportunity to grow into the likeness of God. That process of ever-increasing holiness cannot be undertaken without the Holy Spirit because the Spirit is the one who makes things holy. As Gregory of Nyssa put it, 'whatever is lovely and good originates in God, comes through the Son and is perfected through the Spirit.'[10]

This is part of the Cappadocians' argument for the full divine nature of the Spirit who should be worshipped along with the Father and the Son. Their opponents the Macedonians, named after a bishop of Constantinople who took this view, had argued that, because the Spirit is often named third in line after the Father and the Son, it must be less divine than they are. Worship might be offered *in* the Spirit but should not be offered *to* the Spirit. Yet, for the Cappadocians, this work of perfecting in holiness, bringing creation to its full maturity and completion, is vital, every bit as much a part of creation as the original will and action that brought it into being, that the Spirit *must* be divine along with the Father and Son. In fact, although we might conceptually divide the work of creation into these three – the original will to create, bringing it into being, and the work of completing it – it is in reality one work, one indivisible creative act. This is a form of continuous creation, of creation not yet complete, which incidentally fits well with an evolutionary view of the natural world yet also argues for the Spirit's equality with the Father and Son as involved in the work of creation.

The world is created good, but not yet complete. Like a baby that has to grow into maturity, creation also needs to be developed, to emerge, to evolve. What is true of the whole of creation is also true of human beings, yet is complicated by our own fallen nature. Not only do we need to grow into maturity but we also need to be healed from the damaging spiritual, psychological and moral effects of sin and evil in our hearts and lives. Without the Spirit, we remain unhealed, static and unmoved. We lack the divine energy we were made to enjoy, which brings us healing and draws us towards God's future. This growth in holiness is described by the Cappadocians as *theosis* – growing into or sharing the divine nature (2 Peter 1.4). Humanity was always meant to cooperate with this work of the Holy Spirit – to enable creation to develop and grow into maturity.

We stand under the divine command both to work the creation and to take care of it (Gen. 2.15). The human calling in relation to creation is twofold. First, it is to develop creation, using its resources to bring prosperity and wellbeing to living things. This encompasses all of human ingenuity in technology and art. So, in harmony with the Spirit, we make machines and devices that harvest the fruit of the earth, that bring health where it is lacking and that ease the burden of hard labour that all this involves. We also create artistic representation out of the pigments of colour or the stone or bronze found in the earth – objects of beauty that bring joy.

Second, our call is to 'take care' of creation to ensure it does not decay or dissolve as a result of the call to 'work' the planet and to prevent the harm that creation can do – to develop early warning systems for coming earthquakes for example, or to preserve species of animal life that might be destroyed by others. All this is our work in step with the Spirit who brings life. Our art and technology at their best are a response to and inspired by the Spirit who brings creation to its fulfilment.

Of course, we have failed in this calling. In our hubris, we have developed industrial technologies that do not preserve but instead are gradual destroying this beautiful world. The delicate balance that holds our planet together and enables it to breathe and thrive is unravelling due to our carelessness.

Reversing this seems a huge challenge, and one on which we have made very little progress so far despite our efforts in recycling and reduction of our use of fossil fuels. As we see the torrent of plastic clogging up our oceans, and despite attempts to reduce its use, our seemingly total dependence upon materials that will take centuries to biodegrade makes it hard not to despair at the huge task facing the human race.

This theology of the Holy Spirit, the giver of life at work in all of creation to bring it to its divinely appointed fulfilment, tells us that we are not alone in this task. It tells us that, underneath the human destruction of the planet, there is a deeper power at work restoring, refreshing and drawing creation towards its future. Despite our destructive efforts, trees continue to grow where they can put down roots, rain falls and rivers flow. The earth's wounds heal. Our urgent task is to be filled with the Spirit (Eph. 5.18) and to work in step with the Spirit (Gal. 5.25) who gives life to all living things, rather than to work against that same Spirit who pulsates with growth and fertility.

Care for creation, which, according to Genesis, is a human calling rather than just a narrowly Christian one, is a burden we do not bear alone. To carefully balance the development of technology with care for the planet is part of our purpose here on earth. Whether it is developing machinery to improve transport, working in healthcare, creating a sculpture, tending a garden, refusing to use excessive plastic, or arguing for reduction in emissions – all this is fulfilling our human calling alongside the life of the Spirit who is always at work bringing and giving life.

The Spirit and spirituality

At the same time, one of the other crises facing the human race, particularly in the West, is the increasing polarization and isolation of our societies. As we saw in previous chapters, the breakdown of a common narrative has led us into increasingly small circles of identity without a common story to hold us together. Loneliness is rampant and social isolation is an epidemic. It is said that 9 million people in the UK alone think of themselves as lonely, almost half of those older people.[11]

To remedy our private and mental struggles, we invest in all kinds of spiritual strategies. Spirituality these days is big business. Large companies offer mindfulness courses to employees and there is no shortage of advice on the spiritual side of life in the 'self-help' sections of bookshops. Much contemporary spirituality is precisely this: self-help. It tends, if anything, to be focused on self-realization, the search to discover our own unique, irreducible identity, the search to delve inside and to be ourselves independent of others. As one recent book on the topic puts it, 'Spirituality in its privatized psychological formation is not a cure for our sense of social isolation and disconnectedness, but is, in fact, part of the problem.'[12]

Our contemporary ideas of 'spirit' have their roots partly in the notion of 'spirit' in Aristotle, who relates it primarily to the internal act of thinking – by definition different from anything that is outward, social and physical. Hegel's understanding of Spirit (*Geist*) builds on this to suggest that 'spirit' is not just thinking but thinking that makes itself objective. It is not just abstract thought but comes to actuality in the processes and development of world history. As a culture comes to a certain self-awareness, its 'spirit' is manifested and recognized in cultural achievements and institutions. 'Spirit' is that which is common to all people, the power by which a varied culture comes to understand itself and display its inner reality in history.

This, however, is a long way from the Christian notion of the Holy Spirit, the giver of life, the pulsating, dynamic personal presence at work within the world to bring it to its full maturity. The German theologian Michael Welker describes Hegel's view of spirit and how it is merely descriptive and largely impotent to bring about change: 'it is impossible to see how this spirit could be a power for change, reversal, and new beginning in a situation of spreading individual and collective self-closure and self-production, relatively adjusted and veiled in their brutalities and deficiencies.' Put bluntly, 'Hegelian pneumatology remains simplistic and barren.'[13]

The spirituality of our age tends to be self-focused and all about control. Yet the vision of maturity given in Christian theology to which the Holy Spirit draws us is one where self-realization is found not in discovering our own individual and irreducible difference from everyone else, the search to find ourselves and to be ourselves, but instead is found in learning to become a servant of others and to become people capable not of self-sufficient independence but of building a common life.

Welker points out that, in the Old Testament (for example in the famous story of the dry bones in Ezekiel 37), the particular work of the Spirit is to gather people out of disintegration, distress and insecurity and draw them together to bring them cohesion and purpose.[14] In the Bible, whereas demonic powers isolate and separate people from community, the Spirit brings people together and creates social life by maturing them into those who have been turned outwards from self-absorption and self-interest and instead towards their neighbour. The Spirit is constantly at work to restore community and to renew the forces of life like a garden being refreshed with rain.

Amos Yong offers an intriguing version of Christian orthodoxy, a systematic theology that, at first sight, seems the wrong way round.[15] As a Pentecostal theologian, he starts not, as systematic theologies usually do, with the doctrine of creation, but with the pneumatology, the resurrection and eschatology. A theology based on the Holy Spirit by whom God raised Christ from the dead (Rom. 8.11), will focus first of all on the future towards which the Spirit works to draw us. Reflecting on the letters to the Corinthians, he notices how St Paul combines an emphasis on preaching Christ crucified (1 Cor. 2) with urging the Corinthians to 'pursue love and strive for the spiritual gifts' (1 Cor. 14.1). The apparent incongruity of these two ideas is resolved when we begin to realize the shape of the spiritual life as St Paul envisages it. This 'charismatic theology of the cross' sees *charismata* (spiritual gifts) not as tokens of privilege or power but as 'invitations to bear witness to the coming reign of God . . . in ways that turn this world upside down. Recipients of the charismata, in other words, become servants who build up, edify and encourage others, even if that involves their own self diminishment.'[16]

The pneumatology of Nicaea points in the same direction. The Spirit proceeds from the Father, and the Son is incarnate by the Holy Spirit. As we saw with the Nicene vision of personhood, the Nicene vision of spirituality is one that does not isolate us into individual bubbles of self-sufficient serenity but is the exact opposite of self-help. Where this Holy Spirit has full sway, relationships of mutual giving and receiving result.

If much of our contemporary individualized, customized spiritualities contribute towards the increasing atomization and fragmentation of society, this form of spirituality builds community. Just as the Holy Spirit is at work in the world to renew creation, working to replenish dwindling resources, enabling the natural world to continue to produce fruit and life, working against the efforts of humankind to destroy the planet, so the Holy Spirit is at work among those who open themselves to that same Spirit, to develop habits of compassion and the ability to sacrifice ourselves for the sake of our neighbours, which many contemporary spiritualities are unable to do.

The Spirit and the Church

It is not accidental that, immediately after the article on the Holy Spirit in the Nicene Creed, the reference to speaking through the prophets that carries the implication of the Spirit speaking in and through the authors of Scripture, it goes on to assert, 'we believe in one holy catholic and apostolic Church.'

If the Spirit is at work in the whole of creation to bring it to its fulfilment, then that work is concentrated, as it were, within the life of the Church. At one point, St Basil describes the presence of the Spirit in a person as being like artistic ability. That ability is there at all times, yet occasionally becomes visible and active when the artist starts to paint. In other words, the Christian has the Holy Spirit living within, but the Spirit occasionally becomes visible in words of 'prophecy, healings or other wonderful works'.[17] The same analogy can work for the presence of the Spirit in creation and the Spirit's work in the Church. The Spirit, who is the giver of life, is concentrated in the life of the Church and the people gathered in the name of Christ seek to attune themselves to the work of the Spirit of Christ among them.

So, the Church is not just a place of words. When the Church gathers to break bread and pour out wine in its regular re-enactment of the Last Supper, it does so not just as a bare memory of Jesus. When the Holy Spirit is called down upon these gifts, they do, in some true sense, become the body and blood of Christ for us. When we pray over water, invoking the Holy Spirit and asking that those who are washed in it may be born again into life with Christ, in some profound way, that is exactly what happens: a washing that becomes a 'baptism for the forgiveness of sins' as the Nicene Creed puts it. When we lay hands on someone, praying for them to be filled with the Holy Spirit or confirmed by that Spirit, we trust that this actually takes place. When we pray, these are not just pious hopes, a list of requests wistfully voiced into the air, but the Spirit weaves these words into divine action as one of the ways God achieves his purposes in the world. When a preacher gets up to speak and prays for the Holy Spirit to work through the message, in some mysterious way, God speaks through those very words as the Spirit 'spoke through the prophets'.[18] When words of blessing are spoken over a couple at a wedding, the relationship becomes so much more than just two people who make a commitment to stay together for life. It pictures the goal of human life as fellowship with God in a lifelong, intimate communion, bringing together difference in the coming together of two representatives of the constituent parts of humanity, male and female, out of which union new life can emerge. As vows are spoken and the Spirit is invoked over those vows, a new reality comes into being, what Dietrich Bonhoeffer called 'God's holy ordinance, by means of which he wills to perpetuate the human race until the end of time.'[19]

Again, we see how a generous orthodoxy expands our horizons and the significance of human action.

The Spirit as Gift

The enticing drama of orthodoxy issues a standing invitation to the whole of the human race to allow ourselves to be drawn into the love of God out of which the world was born. It is to be filled with the Spirit and to keep in step as this same Spirit seeks to renew the face of the earth: 'When you send forth your Spirit, they are created; and you renew the face of the ground' (Ps. 104.30).

At the heart of this vision, the article on the Holy Spirit fills out who we are with a little more clarity. We are simple recipients, grateful receivers of the gifts of God. The Spirit is named in the Nicene Creed as the 'giver of life' – the Giver and the Gift.

The Church is reminded to keep asking for the gift of the Spirit because the presence of the Spirit in the Church is the presence of God's free gift to us. It does this when it prays 'Come, Holy Spirit' over the bread and wine of the Eucharist, over the water of baptism, over people seeking confirmation of their faith and wanting to live the fullness of the Christian life, over people seeking prayer and help when they are out of their depth, or offering themselves for ordination. This is a gift that is never received once and for all. It can seem odd that we are to continue to ask for the Spirit. Surely a gift is either given or it isn't? Yet this idea that we need to keep asking every day to be filled with the Holy Spirit preserves two vital perspectives.

The first is that we cannot become who we are meant to be on our own. The Christian life is not a life of strenuous moral effort. There is work to be done, spiritual disciplines to be adopted and projects to be planned, but these are the channels through which the life of the Spirit flows, not the flow of life itself. 'Apart from me', says Jesus, 'you can do nothing' (John 15.5). St Basil says, 'it is impossible to maintain a life of holiness without the Spirit'[20] and, 'if you remain outside the Spirit, you cannot worship at all . . . It is impossible for you to recognize Christ, the image of the invisible God, unless the Spirit enlightens you.'[21] Without the Spirit, we simply cannot live the Christian life however hard we try.

We sometimes think that anything to do with the Holy Spirit (or the Holy Ghost, as we used to say) is a little bit odd, perhaps okay for Pentecostals but not for others. Someone who is completely filled with the Spirit would surely seem very weird. In one sense, that is true. Judged by the standards of the culture of our age, someone glowing with this Holy Spirit, the Spirit of pulsating life, the Spirit that enables us to forget ourselves in the best sense of that word so that we can truly love our neighbour, or even our enemy, and care passionately about the wellbeing of all creation, would seem, like St Francis and all the saints, very weird. Yet, in another sense, if the Spirit is the one who enables us to become who we were created to be in Christ, the Spirit is the one who makes us normal, not conforming to any particular social or cultural expectation of normality but the way we were meant to be. In fact, we cannot become properly normal without the Holy Spirit.

The other reason why the Church has to continually ask for the Spirit is that the Spirit, as the giver of life, is always Gift and never possession. We can never say finally that we possess the Spirit in that the Spirit is never under our control (John 3.8) and always the gift of God to us.[22] The Spirit always has this elusive quality, never nailed down, never fully understood and mastered. The Spirit always moves ahead of us, although never ahead of Christ. There is always more of God to be discovered because, if the Spirit's work is to draw us into the love between the Father and the Son and to find our healing and completion in that love, then we can never, in this life, get to the bottom of it. In fact, as the Cappadocians would tell us, heaven itself will be an on-going journey into the heart of that love.

At the end of the day, we are not self-sufficient, nor were we ever meant to be. We are dependent on God and on each other. We need to receive the gift of the Holy Spirit daily to be all that we have the potential to be. Without that Spirit, we will turn inwards upon ourselves and finally vanish. The Spirit as the giver of life reminds us that we are simply the recipients of gifts. Martin Luther put it well in his last written sentence before he died: 'We are beggars. That is the truth of it.'[23]

In this third article of the creed, we see again what can only be described as a truly generous orthodoxy. We find our vision of life enlarged, the potential for humankind expanded, our understanding of creation and its destiny enlightened and our vision of what happens in church enriched.

The heart of orthodoxy is the generosity of God. It describes this God who constantly goes out from himself, eternally in the begetting of the Son and the procession of the Spirit. With the article on the Spirit, we see ourselves being invited into the intimacy at the heart of God to share his nature of generous-hearted life.

The goal of orthodoxy is not just right belief, but generous people. If we live in a world gifted to us by God, if the Spirit is the giver of life, then those gifts were never meant to rest with us. The mutual nature of human life and society mean they are to be constantly in circulation, passed on to others, as we shall explore more fully in Chapter 10. Our problem is that we so often receive the gifts of God, the gifts of life, the gifts of creation as if they were meant to end up with us, satisfied in our possession of more and more things. Yet the work of the Spirit is precisely this transformation of heart, soul and mind so that we become people capable of not holding on to the gifts we are given, but passing them on to others who also need them in a process of circulation that binds us more strongly to each other in love and dependence and that creates harmonious lives and societies.

Part 2

THE ORTHODOXY
OF GENEROSITY

6

The anatomy of generosity

So far, we have been exploring the generosity of orthodoxy – the idea that Christian orthodoxy as laid out in the Catholic creeds gives us a bigger, richer picture of the world that makes plain what is hidden, draws out its colours, renders it more vivid and yet guards us from its dangers.

At this point, we move on to consider the orthodoxy of generosity. In this chapter, I want to look at the significance of generosity, which both lies at the heart of orthodoxy and is the only appropriate response to it.

G. K. Chesterton, writing about the Christian faith he had gradually discovered as he emerged into adulthood, described it as the 'thrilling romance of orthodoxy'. He went on: 'people have fallen into a foolish habit of speaking of orthodoxy as something heavy, humdrum, and safe. There never was anything so perilous or so exciting as orthodoxy.'[1]

In a brief article called 'The Dogma is the Drama', Dorothy Sayers once described how quite a few people in Britain in the 1940s disliked Christianity without having the faintest idea of what it actually was. 'Many people', she wrote, 'simply cannot believe that anything so interesting, so exciting, and so dramatic could be the orthodox creed of the church.'[2] Both she and Chesterton express in prose far better than mine the sheer wonder of the story the creeds tell and their world-shattering character.

'The Christology of Nicaea' may not sound an exciting topic but it contains a revolutionary idea. The idea is that God has given us not just a world to live in, food on our tables each day, prophets to teach us or a book to guide us, but he has given us nothing less than himself. Islam, for example, is an extraordinarily rich tradition of wisdom, reflection and devotion to God. At its heart is the idea that God has revealed his will to us through the prophet Muhammad in a book, the Qu'ran, which tells how to worship and how to live in submission to God. Allah sends a prophet yet Islam would never dare to claim that God *himself* has come to us. How could he if he is *al-Ahad*, the indivisible One without differentiation, or if there is 'only one God – far be it from his glory that he should have a Son.'[3]

Arius' God sends us help. Jesus as the incarnate created Word battles through the path of moral advancement, obeying God and hence providing us with the prototype and example for us to follow, summoning us to be sons of God just like him.[4] But again, Arius stops short of saying God gives *himself* to us. Yet this is what Nicaea meant by the scandalous claim that the 'only Son of God, eternally begotten of the Father . . . of one being with the Father . . . for us and for our salvation came down from heaven . . . and was made man.' In Jesus Christ, God himself comes to our rescue even though it costs him his life. The playwright has stepped on to his own stage, the unseen Creator of all that we can see and all that we can't once showed his face.

The God of the Macedonians also reaches out to help. He sends us the Spirit, a ministering angel, to help us, but it is only the Spirit described by Basil and Gregory who can do the work that only God can do: perfecting human nature and enabling us to become all we have the potential to be. And this is all on top of the gift of creation that supports our feet as we walk, that offers us every breath in our lungs, that supplies us with food to sustain our bodies and family and friends to bring us joy.

Throughout the Nicene Creed, therefore, we have this pattern of divine generosity and self-giving. Within the life of God himself, as we have seen, there is this pattern of mutual giving and receiving where the Father begets the Son, the Spirit proceeds from the Father and the Son is born of the Spirit through Mary the God-bearer all within the life of the one God.

This highlights the centrality of the idea of Gift, or generosity, at the heart of Nicene credal orthodoxy. The phrase 'generous orthodoxy' might have been a casual remark by Hans Frei picked up by

others over the years, but perhaps it captures the nature of orthodoxy more than he, or others, for that matter, have grasped so far.

Grace and the Gift

A number of scholars in recent times have focused on the centrality
of the idea of 'Gift' in early Christian faith. In particular, John
Barclay has shone a spotlight on the importance of this notion at
the heart of St Paul's understanding of the Christian revolution.[5]

Barclay draws attention to the difference between a payment
and a gift. When a payment is made for services rendered, that
completes the transaction. When someone comes to clean my
windows, I pay them for the job done and that's it. Both parties are
equally satisfied, me with my clean windows, the cleaner with his
or her pay, and we go our own separate ways. A gift, however, is
voluntary and personal. It does not end the transaction but opens
out the relationship to continued reciprocity.

In most societies, gifts expect some kind of return and create
a cycle of reciprocal exchange. When we give a gift at Christmas,
invite someone for a meal or buy someone a drink, these are not
contracts in that they don't legally bind the other person to recip-
rocate. They don't have to give a return gift, and we can't complain
if they don't – after all, there may be very valid reasons why they
can't. However, a gift does carry with it an unspoken expectation
that the other person will respond in some way. Gifts create a cycle
of benevolence that is not enforced by legal sanction but generates
creative relationships of grace and generosity as we try to imagine
new ways to express gratitude.

First-century Greek and Roman culture was organized around
a competition for honour and respect. Gifts and favours were
a common way of lubricating social relationships and, in that
context, gifts would be only given to those who were deemed
worthy of the donor's generosity. The assumption was that those
gifts would be reciprocated to cement alliances, create relationships
and enhance a person's social standing and respect within wider
society. Roman citizens would not generally give gifts to the poor

because they could not return the gift, which would lead to embarrassment all round.

For St Paul, however, God's gift of Jesus Christ had been given irrespective of the worthiness of the recipients. All were now invited into God's covenant with Israel – men and women, slaves and free, Romans and Greeks to join the Jews. Ethnicity, gender, wealth or status counted for nothing in this act of God in Jesus Christ. This was a gift of grace that paid no attention to the worth of the recipient, although it did still expect a response and a change of life – it was unconditioned but not unconditional. Like the gifts we have been discussing, it set up relationships of gratitude, obligation and reciprocity between us and God. This was the radically new message of the gospel: that the grace of the God of Israel was now available to all people and that the Spirit had now been given even to Gentiles who did not possess the Law (Gal. 3.2).

Cultural, gender and social difference are not erased by this gift, but they are relativized. This was Paul's 'attempt to rethink human identity and worth on the basis of a singular, unconditioned gift, which undercuts all other reckoning of worth and gives the only worth that counts.'[6]

The churches that St Paul founded across the Mediterranean world were new, experimental communities based not on gift-giving that greased the wheels of the social hierarchy but a new way of relating. They were founded not on the capital of ethnic, gender or social status but on recognizing each other as recipients of the free gift of God in Christ, and the new patterns of gratitude and obligation that the gift generated. It was not ethnicity, status or wealth but the gracious gift of God that was the currency that mattered in these new communities on the edge of empire. This just didn't fit with the normal categories of honour, gift and race at the time.

This helps explain why St Paul was so determined to ensure that the gift from the Gentile churches arrived at the cash-strapped Jerusalem church (see 2 Cor. 9). In his world riven by ethnic divides – particularly, for him, the great divide between Jew and

Gentile – this was the perfect way to demonstrate the nature and impact of the gospel. This was a gift that mirrored the gift of Christ, expressed the gratitude of Gentiles for the invitation into the covenant with Israel and which created relationship between these two groups – Jews in Jerusalem and Gentiles in the Roman province of Macedonia – that would otherwise have been deeply suspicious of each other. It was a response to God's 'indescribable gift' (2 Cor. 9.15) in Christ that created reciprocity and a positive mutual indebtedness.

Becoming givers

In a related way, Miroslav Volf explores the centrality and dynamics of giving and forgiving in Christian faith.[7] Paganism was based on a bargain with God where offering worship to one of the pagan gods was a means of ensuring favour on yourself and your family. By contrast, in Christian understanding, we cannot give anything to God that is not his to begin with. However, the main thrust of Volf's argument is that the purpose of divine giving is not just so that we can receive God's gift but so that we can become givers ourselves. 'The true God gives so we can become joyful givers and not just self-absorbed receivers.'[8] Divine generosity creates big-hearted people.

Like Barclay, Volf stresses the reciprocity of giving and the way in which an economy based on gift creates relationship.[9] Both insist that God is neither a stingy negotiator driving a hard bargain with us, his creation, nor a divine Santa Claus giving liberally without any ongoing conditions or demands. For Volf, God's gifts create obligations of faith, gratitude, availability and, most of all, participation in the on-going process of giving. He distinguishes between three different ways of approaching possessions: taking (grabbing for ourselves what is not ours), getting (legitimately earning our keep by work done or money spent) and giving (giving favours we don't owe to the undeserving). The purpose of God's gifts is that we learn to imitate him in doing more of the last of these and, in the process, become joyful givers. We are to be the channels of God's gifts so that they pass through us and on to others. Sure, we are to enjoy the gifts of God, but they are not meant to end up with us, festering through disuse. Instead, he envisages a reciprocal circulation of gifts in society that create bonds between us that taking and getting can never create.

Restoring the balance

St Basil the Great had something similar in mind. In his context of frequently famine-hit Cappadocia in the fourth century, holding on to possessions when your neighbour needs them is simply a lack of love. One of the chief sins he identified among his Christian listeners was that of hoarding or storing wealth. Basil aims at what has been called an 'ethic of sustainability', in other words, a way of life that supports the whole of a community and not just a few wealthy people. While he recognizes some will always be wealthier than others, Christian discipleship involves a simplicity of life that is not too bothered about extravagance or consumption but much more about ensuring resources remain in constant circulation. As he preached in one of his sermons:

> Wells become more productive if they are drained completely, while they silt up if they are left standing. Thus wealth left idle is of no use to anyone, but put to use and exchanged it becomes fruitful and beneficial for the public.[10]

Basil often reflects on the economy of the gospel, which is based on the generosity of God where what you hoard turns bad and what you give away comes back to you many times over. This is deeply counter-intuitive in that, rather than focusing on security and stability by acquiring enough money to have a safe nest egg for the future, to secure a good home and achieve our dreams, in the kingdom of God it is what we give away that gets multiplied: 'When wealth is scattered in the manner which our Lord directed, it naturally returns, but when it is gathered it naturally disperses. If you try to keep it you will not have it; If you scatter it you will not lose it.'[11] Likewise, Basil advises Christian investors with spare cash:

> Give away that portion of your silver that is lying idle, do not burden it with interest rates, and it shall be well for you both. You will have the certainty that your money is well guarded, while the one who receives it will have the profit from its use. If you must seek a return on your investment, be satisfied with what comes from the Lord; he himself will pay the additional amount on behalf of the poor.[12]

This constant recirculation of resources where we give what we don't need to others who do need it, restores the balance (*epanisoun* is the Greek word he uses) of an unequal world that always tends to see wealth concentrated in a few hands. Basil has radical things to say to the rich, yet his answer to inequality is not so much taxation but willing generosity as a core element of Christian life.

Each of these ancient and modern authors have noticed the centrality of generosity to both the nature of the gospel and our response to it. This practical focus upon generosity as central to Christian living arises out of the immanent Trinity, the relations between the divine persons where, as Miroslav Volf puts it:

> each loves and glorifies the other two, and each receives love and glory from them . . . all give in the eternally moving circle of exchanges. And, because they give in this way, they have all things in common except that which distinguishes them from each other. [13]

Yet this dynamic in the immanent Trinity finds expression in the divine economy, in time and history, in the extraordinary gift of creation, in the coming into the world of the incarnate Son Jesus and the gift of the Holy Spirit. This is a world that lives and breathes Giftedness and generosity if only we have eyes to see it, and we are invited to join in this constant rhythm of exchange.

Generosity and orthodoxy

With all this in mind, we can perhaps begin to see that generosity and orthodoxy are not in opposition, or even in tension with each other, but that the one describes the other. True orthodoxy is generous and generative both in the scope it gives to explore the expanded universe that belief in the God of Nicaea gives us, and in that it has generosity, grace and Gift at its very heart. The God that orthodoxy describes is none other than a God of grace and Gift.

When we grasp this, the only proper response to this God who gives himself to us in Christ is a corresponding generosity. We love because God loved us. We give because God first gave to us. As we are drawn into this cycle of giving, we gradually learn to let go of the things we cling to that we think will give us security. We begin to realize that our true security comes to us as a gift from God himself and that, while a basic level of income is needed, our trust in wealth and possessions to give us security for the future is misplaced. Having a large bank balance is no protection against sickness, family breakdown or a scandal that ruins a life. It certainly is no protection against death.

We might even describe the heart of sin as a refusal of the gift of God and a consequent resistance to the pattern of generosity that it generates. We are told in the Gospels that the only unforgivable sin is the sin against the Holy Spirit (Mark 3.29). This is the rejection of the gift of the Spirit who alone can draw us into the life of God, the refusal to join in the cycle of grace and gratitude that keeps the world thriving and, instead, insisting on holding on to what we have, refusing to recognize this deep structure of the world and shutting ourselves out of the cycle of Gift, grace and gratitude.

The purpose of God's gift is to recreate us as generous people, to loosen the grip of fear, acquisitiveness and greed which eats away at our souls and, instead, to learn the delightful freedom of giving and the simplicity of knowing that our most basic needs are supplied by the God who clothes the flowers of the field and counts the sparrows. The world as revealed through the lens of the Nicene

Creed is one that has Gift and grace at its very centre. Creation and Incarnation are gifts from a God who invites us into relationships of giving and receiving: receiving from God and then learning to give and receive to and from each other.

The extraordinary ordinary

If grace and generosity are at the heart of both the gospel and our response to it, then this has implications for Christian spirituality and discipleship, implications that arise out of the Christology we have been exploring, especially when we follow the debate a century or so after Nicaea.

We have already touched on the lengthy and complex debates that ensued after Nicaea leading up to the Council of Constantinople in 381 AD. Looking back, that was perhaps the triumph of Nicene orthodoxy, however it didn't solve or resolve all the Church's theological debates around the person of Christ. It was one thing to assert that the Son of God was 'of one being with the Father' but that then left open the question of how divinity and humanity are related in Christ. If he is both human and divine, how on earth (or even in heaven) could we conceive of such a thing? If God and creation are utterly different from one another, how could they possibly coincide in one person? It would be like combining stone and water, something that is just impossible to imagine.

This is the story that leads up to the Council of Chalcedon in 451 AD, which did not produce a new creed – it was felt that Nicaea was perfectly adequate – but sought to define more closely some of the mysteries that Nicaea had left unaddressed.

To cut a long story short, in the intervening years, a number of different Christological options to solve this problem were tried and rejected. Perhaps we should imagine a human body with a divine soul, as Apollinarius thought? But that left the human soul untouched by God and unredeemed. Another option was to preserve the integrity of Christ by imagining a kind of blend of humanity and divinity into one unique being, an idea put forward by Eutyches, a priest and monk from Constantinople. In this view, humanity and divinity are combined like wine and water in a jar so that what results is a blended substance that is neither proper wine nor proper water. The opposite suggestion came from Nestorius, Archbishop in Constantinople in the late 420s, who thought it vital to preserve the full humanity of Christ. He argued that Christ's human nature could not be preserved unless it was quite distinct from his divine nature, although the two were united in the same person. With this idea, humanity and divinity are united in Christ a bit like oil and water poured together into a jar. They form a kind of unity within the one space, but they do not blend in any way and remain separate.

The Council of Chalcedon rejected the suggestions of both Nestorius and Eutyches. Nestorius' version was inadequate because it implied two entirely separate natures within the same person, one divine and one human. It implied that human nature remained distinct and so could not in any way be transformed from within by the divine nature in Christ. Eutyches' doctrine implied that, because the Son's human and divine nature were fused together, what resulted was neither fully human nor fully divine. Like a centaur which was half man and half horse, it was neither one thing nor the other. Christ cannot really sympathize with us in our weakness but neither can he really bring God to us in the way that Nicaea had insisted was vital for salvation.

The Chalcedonian definition repeated the *homoousios* from Nicaea, but extended it to say that the Son was *homoousios* (of the same nature) not just with God but with us, so that Jesus Christ was to be

> recognized in two natures, without confusion, without change, without division, without separation; the distinction of natures being in no way annulled by the union, but rather the characteristics of each nature being preserved and coming together to form one person and subsistence.

This definition rejected the idea that Jesus was half human and half divine as Nestorius seemed to suggest. It also rejected the

Eutychian notion that he is a hybrid conglomeration of the two which is neither human nor divine. Instead, it insisted he is 100 per cent human like us and 100 per cent divine like the Father and the Spirit.

In other words, in Jesus, we see God living and working through a fully human life. This is God doing what he does through the entire human nature of Jesus. It is not as if Jesus did his miracles and was raised from the dead in his divine nature while leaving his humanity to do the ordinary things like eat, sleep, carve tables, walk with friends, endure suffering and manage the usual struggles of human life. When people met Jesus, there was no halo or gentle glow to indicate that he was different yet, for those with eyes to see it, Jesus' divine nature was working through his human nature at every single point. So, in walking on the lake, raising dead bodies, multiplying food and knowing the future before it happened, yet also in drinking wine, talking with friends, growing up in a family, paying taxes and suffering on the cross, all of this is God doing divine work through human nature. It is God experiencing the weakness of human life. It is humanity seeing, for once, what it is to have divine life coursing through every part of a human heart and mind. This is a picture of what a God-shaped human life or, to put it better, what true human life looks like.

True spirituality?

Now, all this has something to say to our concepts of spirituality and wellbeing today. Much contemporary spirituality suggests that wisdom is to be found by transcending the body to reach some higher state of awareness that lifts us out of the ordinary stuff of life. Or it suggests that our true identity is found in some inner essence of ourselves rather than in our embodied nature or our social relations. In this approach, we find out who we really are not by identifying ourselves by our relationships with family, community or associations but instead by discerning some inner, psychologically defined self where our instincts and desires are the most foundational thing about us.

The Freudian move to identify those inner desires, most importantly sexual ones, as the most fundamental drivers for action is part of the same turn away from socially defined notions of identity. It is a turn away from seeing ourselves as externally defined – as essentially neighbours, citizens, parents, children or friends – and instead seeing ourselves as beings whose true nature is independent from these messy factors of ordinary life – family, community or *polis*. Even in the Church, spirituality can sometimes be seen as confined to, or most intensely present in, ecstatic experiences, contemplative moments or spiritual retreats that have little to do with the give and take, the ordinary transactions of everyday living. Even our technology joins in with this in the development of artificial intelligence that seeks to create forms of life and intelligence independent of physicality.

In these approaches, various kinds of ascetic practise or spirituality are seen as either escaping from the limitations of or transcending physical, bodily life. This was the mistake of Gnosticism, which we have seen the early Church reject as sub-Christian. Much of it was based on the rejection of the goodness of a physical creation and instead the idea that redemption was salvation *from* the body rather than salvation *of* the body. For example, for the Valentinians, one of the most popular Gnostic systems, Christ comes to earth with a body that is not fully human like ours and only to redeem the spirit, not the flesh.

Irenaeus, in contrast, saw true spirituality as arising out of the recapitulation, or re-enactment as it were, of the whole of human life in Christ. For him, as for the whole Nicene tradition, the Incarnation has to touch every part of human life. Christ has to be fully human – mind, soul, body, spirit and everything else – if all of human life is to be redeemed. That is why Apollinarius' idea that the human soul was replaced in Christ by a divine soul didn't work: it meant that the soul was untouched by God's presence and therefore not transformed by it. It is why Nestorius' dualism didn't work either: it left human nature untouched and unredeemed because it was kept distinct from his divine nature.

The vision that Irenaeus, Athanasius and the Cappadocians were striving for is of a humanity transformed just like a sick body injected with antibiotics that heal every part of the body, not leaving some parts of it still ailing. The Son, by being 'made man', fully human yet fully divine, redeems every aspect of human life – not just the spiritual aspect of it – in a way that doesn't allow us to leave behind ordinary things like money, homes, cities, food and possessions as basically irrelevant to the spiritual life.

Christology and spirituality

If a Chalcedonian Christology is in any way right, it is precisely in these things and our use of them that true spirituality is worked out. The ordinary limitations of life, the fact that we have to go to work, pay bills, get on with awkward neighbours, grow and get older – these are not things to be left behind or ignored in the attainment of true spiritual growth but are the very conditions and contexts in which spiritual growth happens.

The Christ of Nicaea and Chalcedon is a vision of the whole of human life transfigured and transformed from within by divine presence. It is a life lived not on some higher plane of enlightenment but in the context of first-century village life – brothers arguing over inheritance, seed scattered across the ground, Roman imperial might, Jewish hopes for the future. These mundane realities are not left behind as unimportant to the true spiritual seeker but are transformed and enlarged, their significance enriched in the presence of Jesus. A meeting between Jesus and a young Jewish fisherman becomes a revelation of the Son of God. An encounter with a distraught widow at a funeral procession for her son leads to a signpost to the resurrection at the end of time. A hungry crowd desperate for food turns into a glimpse of God's abundant generosity in the creation of all things. A storm on a lake becomes a vision of God's final triumph over chaos.

The spirituality of Nicene Christology does not offer an escape from the ordinary political and social contexts that we have to deal with but transfigures them from within. This is Nicene and

Chalcedonian Christology made visible. It is the Spirit giving life to all created things so that, as Michael Welker puts it, the illumination of the Spirit is about more than ecstatic experience. It means 'nothing less than that real fleshly life is enabled by the Spirit and in the Spirit to be the place where God's glory is made present'.[14] In this vision of life, every aspect of our bodily life – waking, sleeping, food, sex, voting, bank balances, local and national politics – are to be conformed to Christ and the pattern of life we see in him because, in him, we see the totality of human life transformed by the divine presence in every part.

Thus, there is no part of life that is left untouched by and independent of Christ's claim upon it. The spiritual life, the vision of life given us by the creeds, is lived precisely in the conditions and limitations of everyday, ordinary existence. As Luke Bretherton puts it:

> The spiritual battle is fought not in some ethereal, otherworldly realm, but in the shaping and actions of our everyday life. Who eats at our table, what we eat, where our money is invested, how we conduct ourselves in relation to our spouse, or children or neighbour or enemy: this is the cosmic arena in which we play our part in God's will being done and the birthing of God's Kingdom come.[15]

Our experiences of the Spirit, whether in eucharistic celebration, the felt presence of God in worship, the transformative power of prayer ministry, or contemplative prayer, are given to confirm, inspire, encourage and motivate us for the ordinary tasks of life. They help us see our friends and neighbours differently in the light of Christ. Those experiences open our eyes in a very powerful way to the bigger reality opened up to us, the 'things unseen', so that we can learn to notice that reality in more ordinary encounters.

Christology, creation and generosity

To return to the main theme of this chapter, one of the main ways in which this works out is generosity. If the spiritual life is lived out in the give and take of everyday transactions – how we spend our money, what we do with our homes, what we do with our spare time – then a crucial test of faith will not be whether we can rattle off items of credal belief (although, as we have seen, theological precision does matter), nor whether we have powerful encounters with the Spirit (although these can also be transformative for faith) but rather whether we have the ability to give generously of our time, money, mercy and forgiveness.

In a culture that tends to believe that we need to acquire the resources that will enable us to live our dream – that a successful and good life is marked by prosperity, wealth and comfort, that we will find happiness by independence from others rather than interdependence – generosity or the art of giving is a radically counter-cultural act.

A person who has learned to let go of what our culture tells us is essential, the stuff we supposedly cannot live without, is someone who has begun to understand the nature and beauty of Christian orthodoxy because they have come to see that the heart of this life, this created reality in which we find ourselves, is pure Gift.

So often, our national and personal economies are dominated by an ideology of scarcity. We don't have enough to go around, so we cling to what we have and we build bigger barns to provide us with security for the future. Yet, if we are navigating life by the map of Christian orthodoxy, it tells us we live in a world of grace, of abundance not scarcity. It tells us of a God who 'is able to provide you with every blessing in abundance, so that by always having enough of everything, you may share abundantly in every good work' (2 Cor. 9.8).

Generosity flowers in the soil of a theology of abundance rather than scarcity. If the world simply evolved out of primeval micro-organisms or fields of energy by pure chance, there is no sense of Gift in it because there is no Giver. If the world is the creation of a God who is in himself a life of constant Gift and continues to give everything that sustains life each day, then this is the way the world works and everything is freely given and received. If you are competing for scarce resources, when you give something away, you lose it. Yet, in the kingdom of God, when you give away, you gain: 'the one who sows sparingly will also reap sparingly, and the one who sows bountifully will also reap bountifully . . . You will be enriched in every way for your great generosity, which will produce thanksgiving to God through us' (2 Cor. 9.6,11).

So many of our anxieties are related to money, whether the prospect of poverty (despite the fact that it constitutes the experience of most Christians in the world today) or the anxieties that come with having too much to know what to do with. Wealth tends to get a grip on our hearts so that, unless it is regularly given away and used, it ends up possessing us rather than us possessing it. The more we know the endlessly generous God described in the creeds, the more we find release from the grip of the power of wealth on our hearts.

7
Heresy

We come to the opposite of orthodoxy: heresy. In the introduction to this book, we imagined a series of islands, one of which was a broad, welcoming space, but with sheer cliffs on all sides. A good place to be with much to explore and to enjoy, but with limits and dangers at the same time. If orthodoxy is a map to the island of this life that helps us discover its true meaning, explore its hidden glories, appreciate its beauty, and leads us safely to its exit, then heresies might be understood as paths that might initially seem quite attractive, yet lead a bit too close to the edge of the island and, if pursued too far, will lead you over the cliff.

Heresy is not a popular idea these days due to understandable fears that it can be used as a weapon to silence legitimate voices, and we will need to examine why it might still be necessary. However, before we explore that, it's worth trying to define what heresy actually is. Henry Chadwick described a heretic as 'a person wanting to stay within the community while reinterpreting its fundamental documents & beliefs in ways which are unacceptable to the main body, and persisting therein when asked to correct himself.'[1] G. R. Evans argues that 'It is not possible to become a heretic by accident. Heresy involves choice, and perseverance in an opinion when the church has pronounced it wrong.'[2]

These two definitions highlight three key aspects of the meaning of heresy. The first is the element of persistence. Both definitions emphasize that a heresy is not just an ephemeral opinion or a speculative idea expressed in passing. Christian orthodoxy has room for wondering, trying out ideas, weighing them and exploring their implications. After all, it took 300 years and all kinds of thought experiments and intense discussion to come up with the

Nicene Creed. Yet, once the Church has made up its mind, heresy is deliberate persistence in an idea that the Church has decided is a mistake.

The second is the communal nature of orthodoxy. Orthodoxy is what a community decides on as what they believe together. It is, by definition, corporate: it can never be what one individual decides alone. The Nicene Creed, for example, is the result of the deliberations of the bishops gathered in that small town near Constantinople in 325 AD as they hammered out together what they and the Church believed about God and the person of Jesus Christ. It was decided finally by a vote, with just two bishops voting against the final creed and its condemnation of Arian teaching. We might argue that many of them voted that way because they knew the emperor was expecting them to do so but, whatever the motives, the principle remains: that it was decided together. It's significant that we do not know who drafted or wrote any of the Catholic creeds, nor do we need to know, as they are collective documents.[3]

The third and related aspect of the definition of heresy is the element of individual choice involved in it. G. R. Evans highlights the element of choice in holding doggedly to what ends up as heresy. The word 'heresy' comes from the Greek word *haeretidzō* (to choose). That develops into the noun *haeresis*, which can mean a sect or an opinion. Heresy is going it alone, theology done on your own without the corrective and collective wisdom of the wider community, and insisting that you are right, even when most people in the community say you are wrong.

Christians viewed this element of 'choice' differently from the philosophical schools around in the early centuries of the Church. Jane Williams puts it like this:

> The various schools were called 'haereses', or 'choices', suggesting a free market, consumerist approach to reality: choose the one that suits best, and that enables the 'good life' as defined by the chooser. That approach becomes, in Christian discourse, a sign of deviance: 'choice', 'haereses', becomes

'heresy', since to choose for ourselves how we will define reality suggests that there is no given reality, over against us, no one truth, given and held by one God, and therefore not open to the kind of tolerant scepticism that results from this approach to 'generosity'.[4]

Paganism could not sustain much of a notion of heresy as, with numerous gods, it lacked definition and was endlessly diverse. Because the Christians believed in a particular God – the God of Jesus Christ – they had to develop a concept of heresy: understandings of God that were not just interesting options to set alongside others but opinions to be avoided and shunned because they carried dangers.

The heretical imperative

That, of course, raises some interesting issues for us today in a world where individual autonomy and choice is highly prized and usually valued above conformity to the group. We live in a world where heresy, in this sense of individual choice, is not so much discouraged and frowned on but actively encouraged as vital to a thriving society. John Stuart Mill captures the modern distaste for heresy and the valuing of independent thought: 'No-one can be a great thinker who does not recognize that as a thinker it is his first duty to follow his intellect to whatever conclusions it may lead.'[5]

One of the primary virtues of the modern world is authenticity: being true to who you really are inside, 'being yourself' and choosing your own individual path through life. Charles Taylor suggests that the loss of God in modern Western societies has led to the disenchantment of the world, with no external sacred structure to which we need to conform. In turn, this has led to a heightened and self-absorbed individualism, the loss of any higher purpose, the primacy of instrumental, practical reason and therefore the dominance of technology.[6] This 'culture of authenticity', which emerged from the end of the eighteenth century, with its moral demand to be true to ourselves (because there is no truth out there to conform to), means society is effectively neutral on what it is to live a good life, with a 'soft relativism' that means no one has a right to question anyone else's choices. Today, we are all heretics.

To put it differently, if we are all heretics, then none of us are. Except that is not entirely true. There are some ideas and convictions that do continue to carry almost universal value in Western societies. So, for example, to deny the supremacy of democracy as the best (or least worst) form of government is to adopt heresy in modern Western political life. To argue against climate change even though the majority of the world's scientists agree that the evidence is virtually conclusive is, in certain circles, to commit heresy. To deny the Holocaust against the overwhelming evidence of history is a heretical belief. This doesn't stop people believing these things, but to imagine these minority notions may give us a better glimpse of how heresy worked in premodern times. It also helps us see why heresy mattered.

As we have already seen, heresies were not just interesting ideas, an option to believe if you wanted to, but they were actively discouraged, even persecuted, as they were downright dangerous. Today, to argue against democracy might open the door to a totalitarian society. To reject climate change could endanger the future of the planet if it stops us taking the action we need to prevent environmental catastrophe. To deny the Holocaust is perilous as it could make it more possible for something similar to happen again. We can lampoon old obsessions with heresy, but just a little imagination can help us see how our ancestors thought that heresy was not fun, it was serious business. This doesn't excuse some of the ungenerous ways in which Christians have accused each other prematurely of heresy, much less the active persecution and punishment of those deemed heretics, but it does help explain why it was such a big issue.

The value of heresy

Of course, the notion of orthodoxy and heresy has been used in the past to scapegoat and exclude in harmful and capricious ways.

Sometimes, people have been pronounced heretics not because they have offended against the core beliefs of the community but because they offended powerful people and institutions. As Mark Edwards has argued, some beliefs that were later condemned as heresy were deemed orthodox in their own times and, with hindsight, have proved to be building blocks for the emergence of orthodoxy.[7] There are also times when whistle-blowers on corruption have been labelled heretics and even burnt at the stake as a result (the Bohemian Reformer Jan Hus and his execution as a result of the Council of Constance in 1415 comes to mind).[8] But abuse does not deny use. The fact that the notion of heresy has been abused does not mean we can dispense with it any more than we can dispense with the idea of love because many crimes are committed in its name.

The reality is that every society, every organization that has convictions, needs a sense of heresy otherwise it loses its own identity. Western societies are self-defined as democratic, valuing such things as human rights, the environment and the rule of law. To contradict these is to strike at the heart of these societies, as became clear in the reaction to the September 11, 2001 attacks in New York, or the terrorist attacks in London, Madrid and Manchester. In reaction to such attacks, politicians often speak of 'protecting our most cherished values' or 'preserving our way of life'.

In the same way, any organization with a particular identity or set of beliefs needs a sense of heresy. For a member of a left-wing political party, for example, to try to argue for an unfettered free market, for lower taxation or to restrict the powers of trade unions would fall foul of Henry Chadwick's view of heresy outlined above. That would be someone wanting to remain part of their party while at the same time defining that party's core commitments in ways that are out of tune with the core convictions and identity of that party. If they were to adopt those ideas, they would be betraying their most prized values. They would be losing their own soul. Party members who start to entertain such ideas usually end up having to leave the party and join a different one, and the same is true with right-wing parties as well.

Moreover, as Charles Taylor argues, pure choice can never be the last word. The importance of a particular choice is defined by a wider 'horizon of significance'. If the only thing that gives significance is the choice itself, there is no significance. If everything is about the importance of choice in itself, there is no greater significance in choosing justice or injustice, honesty or duplicity, than in choosing pizza or steak for lunch.[9] On the contrary, what we believe matters. We are back to John Webster's reminder of the character of creeds as confessions, acts of allegiance that repudiate the falsehood that threatens the very nature of the community that asserts that creed. Saying 'yes' to truth means saying 'no' to falsehood. As Webster puts it, 'what is so grievous about the loss of an operative notion of heresy is that it is symptomatic of the loss of an operative notion of truth.'[10]

We can perhaps begin to see why the concept of heresy matters and how it preserves a sense of identity and specificity. Heresy is about keeping our very identity. It is about our heart and soul. It is that important. And it helps us see why organizations, whether political parties, campaigning groups or churches, need to fight tooth and nail to keep heresy at bay.

Hunting for heresies is not usually to be recommended. It is well worth remembering that creeds are ultimately more about telling the truth than avoiding mistakes. The pathways through the island are more important than the cliffs at its edge. They are about helping us know and speak the truth rather than just warning us against getting it wrong. It's also worth remembering that there is a difference between heresy and error. It's quite possible to make a theological mistake which is then, in time, recognized as such and turned away from. As we have already seen, orthodoxy is the product of a long process of pondering, praying, worshipping and discerning on behalf of the whole Church. Heresy is something that the community decides as a result of this long process. It is a way of thinking and believing that does not do justice to the true nature of the revelation of God in Jesus Christ through the Holy Spirit. Heresy, as a reminder, is when a person stubbornly holds to an opinion that the rest of the Church has already decided does not work. It is pressing on in the path that is leading towards the edge of the cliff and not turning back even when warned to do so. As G. R. Evans reminded us, you can't become a heretic by accident.

There isn't time or space in this book to explore all of the different heresies that have been identified over the years, but we will look at a selection of Christian ideas deemed heretical to show how they are ultimately destructive not just of Christian faith but of human life and the goodness of creation.

A flawed world

As we saw in Chapter 2, part of the background to the Nicene Creed's assertions that God the Father Almighty is the Creator of heaven and earth and the specific idea of creation *ex nihilo* was the debates over Gnostic ideas that raged through the second century AD.

What has become known as Gnosticism is a dizzyingly complex network of myths and stories giving an account of the origins of the world and the nature of salvation. Its relationship to early Christianity is complex, yet it seems to have emerged not just as a Christian heresy but on the fringes of both Judaism and Christianity, sometimes out of attempts to read the Old Testament in the light of Paul. Included within this broad category are movements eventually recognized as heretical such as Marcionism and Manichaeism. Broadly speaking, these groups believed in an absolutely transcendent and unknown God or Father, sometimes known as the *Pleroma* (fullness). A malfunctioning world such as this could not have been the work of such a God but, in one of the most popular Gnostic myths, was the product of an inferior divinity, the Demiurge, itself the product of Sophia, one of many aeons generated by the Father. This inferior Demiurge created the world from pre-existent matter, assisted by lower angels. To remedy the faults in creation, Sophia had sown the seeds of 'spirit' in the material world. This gave birth to the elect, the sons of God, and gave them *gnosis* (knowledge) that would enable them to escape the physical world of flesh and return to the realm of the unknown God, leaving behind the rest of humanity that continued to live under the oppressive rule of the Demiurge. The final end of history would be the dissolution and destruction of this flawed cosmos.[11]

This was a tempting vision. It offered all the attractions of secret knowledge and the revelation of hidden mysteries in a world where mystery religions were already popular and influential. Yet, in these first few centuries, a number of problems emerged with these ideas that meant they were eventually rejected.

First, they denied the goodness of creation. By asserting that the God who made the world was not God the Father Almighty, the Father of Jesus Christ, Gnostics severed creation and salvation and rendered this world irredeemably flawed and broken. Of course, the orthodox Christian vision also recognized the fractured and damaged nature of this world and yet insisted this was an aberration, the corruption of an originally good and perfect world rather than something that is inherent within the world itself. It also envisaged a renewed and restored creation (a 'new heavens and a new earth, where righteousness is at home', 2 Peter 3.13) rather than its destruction. If salvation effectively means escaping from this world into a spiritual realm elsewhere and the ultimate destruction of this world, then why preserve it? Trashing the planet with greenhouse gases, plastic and the fruits of human consumption is only accelerating the inevitable and there are no real grounds for caring for the planet upon which we live.

Moreover, this was an essentially elitist view of the world. It envisaged a group of select individuals, the Gnostics, who knew the secrets of eternal life and therefore could escape from the distraction of the 'worldly minded'. It left an ethic of avoiding rather than loving your neighbour. The Jesus of the Gnostic Gospel of Thomas is a teacher of wisdom. The document is a collection of sayings, not a narrative of Jesus' life, death and resurrection. Salvation is found in acknowledging his teaching rather than through his death and resurrection, which are simply not in focus. As this Jesus says, 'I disclose my mysteries to those who are worthy of my mysteries' (Gospel of Thomas 62). The emphasis within Gnosticism was not that of an open secret to be shared and communicated with as many people as possible but the secret knowledge that enabled the chosen ones to escape the rest of a flawed humanity and a broken creation into another world.

Gnosticism was also politically quietist. Because salvation consisted of fleeing this world and its physicality, there was no great emphasis on redeeming this world and bringing about any sense of transformation within it. Gnosticism held no challenge to a violent, oppressive empire as it gave no grounds for opposing evil and injustice, simply recommending escape from it. Gnostics did not really create churches in the sense of local communities living out a vision of the future kingdom of God and holding out that hope for the rest of society.

It also raised serious questions about the goodness of God. Despite acquitting the supreme God of responsibility for a flawed creation, the idea that the Demiurge created the world from some pre-existent matter raised the distinct possibility, or even the necessity, that there was some element of God's character that was dark and unknown. As Irenaeus put it:

> within the Father of whom they speak, they should conceive of some place, void, formless and full of darkness in which those things were formed which have been formed. Thus they do introduce defect and error within the Pleroma and into the bosom of the Father.[12]

In short, if the Church had swallowed Gnosticism wholesale, Christianity would have given no grounds for valuing the physical world and would have become more elitist and exclusive, feeling no particular responsibility for the rest of society. It would have had no vision for wider society or call to strive for justice within the world, and would raise doubts over whether we could really trust the God who made us. It would not give us a God who gave us a garden of delight to live in, or would ever come into that world for our sake. It would give us a God who is smaller, meaner, than the God of Christian orthodoxy. This is why early Christian thinkers such as

Irenaeus, Tertullian, Clement and Origen saw this as a dangerous path that would lead us over the cliff edge if followed too far.

Christological alternatives

Just as Gnosticism provides the background for the assertions of the first article of the creed about the Father, the second article of the creed, outlining the identity of Jesus as the only begotten son of God, emerged out of the background of the various Christological debates focused around Arianism. We have already touched upon the insights of George Steiner and Robert Jenson, who questioned how our words and stories can make any meaningful sense if they are not related to an ultimate, overarching story that exists independent of and over our stories, whether there can be any meaning without a prior Word from God to which all our words respond. Yet there is another implication of Arianism, which identified it as a path that would lead into dangerous places.

When the Nicene fathers decided to include the word *homoousios* within the creed, they claimed that the Son who became incarnate shared the very nature of God the Father. They said that Jesus was indeed the image of God and had taken flesh for all humanity. Furthermore, in not shying away from the fact that this same incarnate Christ 'suffered under Pontius Pilate', they claimed that this persecuted, falsely accused, unjustly treated, executed rabbi was, in fact, a revelation of the true God. The Old Testament briefly contained the idea that all human beings are made in the image of God, but the early Christian assertion that Jesus is that true image takes this insight further and gives it shape and deeper significance. It means that the image of God is seen not just in the wealthy or the powerful – the emperor, the well-born or the elite Gnostics – but in all people, even (perhaps especially) the persecuted, the falsely accused and the unjustly treated. This Nicene assertion was a doctrinal expression of the early Christian instinct that brought together a much more varied and less socially stratified form of community than almost any other association in the ancient world.

It wasn't just Arianism either. The trajectory of thought from Nicaea to Chalcedon was also a rejection of Apollinarianism – the idea that, in Jesus, the human soul was replaced by a divine soul in a human body – a rather neat and easily understood way of thinking about the divine and human in Christ. This would have meant little hope for the radical transformation of the human soul, and in those moments when we despair of our repeated failure and inadequacy, there would have been little hope of genuine transformation and change because there would have been no such thing as a human soul transfigured by the divine presence, not even in Christ.

Similarly, Nicaea rejected the Adoptionism of figures such as Paul of Samosata (*c.* 200–275 AD), which was another fairly simple way of solving the Christological problem. It suggested that Jesus was born as an ordinary human yet adopted as the Son of God and infused with the divine Spirit at his baptism, which then enabled him to overcome his faults and sins. Again, there are attractions here. Adoptionism at its best wanted to highlight the Father's active declaration of love for Jesus and emphasize that Jesus was properly human like us.

Yet, as Rachel Muers points out, Adoptionism suggests that God is only provisionally committed to that particular human life at a moment in time. He was not eternally committed to humanity in Christ from the beginning, as the doctrine that God was the eternal Father of the Son suggested. Adoptionism suggests a randomness in God's choice. Like the mysterious hand in a well known advert for the National Lottery in the UK, coming out of the sky and pointing at an individual saying, 'It Could be You!', or Diego Maradona's famous claim that the 'hand of God' helped him score the winning goal for Argentina against England in the 1986 World Cup, so the hand of God happens to alight on Jesus. It could, in principle, have alighted on anyone in that crowd waiting for baptism at the hand of John the Baptist. It stimulates the wistful hope that God's hand might just alight on us. Yet the orthodox take on this is very different and more secure. As Muers puts it:

The word from God at Jesus's baptism, then, doesn't just say 'It could be you, too' to all those people who are standing with Jesus; it says 'Because this person exists, it will be you too.' We don't become children of God separately; we become children of God in relation to the firstborn Son of God. We join a particular family.[13]

If the church had adopted Adoptionism, it would have left us with an anxious hoping that God's favour will alight on us as it did on Jesus. It would have given us a God who is not utterly committed to his human creation, not one who has always been and always will be the loving Father of the Son but a Father who chose to be one at some point and who could conceivably decide not to be Father at another. As with Arianism, it would give us a less generous God, one who does not give us himself but sends someone else instead.

Pelagius or Paraclete?

The third section of the creed on the Spirit, as we saw in the last chapter, took place against the background of the debates of the Cappadocians with the Macedonians: the Spirit-opposers. A classic Christian heresy that wasn't part of that discussion but that emerged in the following century was Pelagianism, named (rather unfairly perhaps, as very often those who get heresies named after them aren't the main culprits) after the British monk Pelagius, who was active in the Church in Rome in the early fifth century. He was a popular spiritual counsellor among the wealthy of Rome who were attracted to the newly popular Christian Church. He was troubled both by the lax approach to Christian discipleship he encountered among Roman Christians and by what he considered the languid quietism of Augustine's prayer 'command what you will, and give what you command',[14] which seemed to emphasize divine grace so much that it left little room for human effort. He emphasized very strongly the power of the human will to attain perfection. Others, such as Caelestius and Julian of Eclanum, took these ideas further to question the notion that the human race was infected with sin from the very beginning in Adam, in a form of perfectionism that demanded nothing less than total dedication to holiness.

Again, as we've seen before, there were great attractions in this. Pelagianism was, to a certain extent, a reforming movement within the Roman church. It offered a serious approach to discipleship, which theologies that emphasize divine grace sometimes struggle to motivate. Pelagius offered a positive view of human capacity and a belief in human freedom and responsibility. There were, to be sure, misunderstandings in this debate, with both Augustine and Pelagius using the same words such as 'grace' and 'nature' but meaning different things by them. But, at the end of the day, Augustine's arguments against the cluster of ideas associated with the name of Pelagius won out, with Pelagianism being condemned as a heresy at the Council of Carthage in 418.

There is a great deal of Pelagianism about and Christianity is often portrayed in Pelagian terms. A British Prime Minister, wanting to encourage Christians one Easter a few years ago, said this: 'Easter is all about remembering the importance of change, responsibility, and doing the right thing for the good of our children. And today, that message matters more than ever.'[15] Having read the New Testament, you would be forgiven for thinking the message of Easter was more about the cross and the resurrection, rather than 'doing the right thing'!

Similarly, we constantly hear the supposedly inspirational idea that the human spirit is so strong that you can achieve anything you want to if you try hard enough. Pelagius himself said something similar in a letter to one of his female Christian followers, Demetrias: 'The best incentive for the mind consists in teaching it that it is possible to do anything which one really wants to do.'[16]

The creed, however, asserts that salvation comes about 'by the power of the Holy Spirit'. It is through the Spirit that Christ 'became incarnate' for our salvation. It was for our sake and for our benefit that he was crucified. All the emphasis is on divine not human activity – on what God does, not what we do.

The trouble with Pelagianism is that it put things the other way round. It lays almost all the emphasis on human effort rather than divine initiative, so that how things turn out is entirely your fault or to your credit. Sin, in this view, is a result of lack of effort. If you do not achieve your dreams, whether moral perfection as Pelagius had in mind, or even a successful job, lots of money, a fancy car and a big house, then there's no one to blame but yourself. You just haven't tried hard enough. It is a classic meritocratic view of the world which, as Michael Sandel has argued, generates divisiveness and resentment, hubris among the winners and harsh judgement on those who have failed.[17] It disregards the uneven nature of society that tilts the balance in favour of some who are born with all kinds of advantages and makes it harder for those born into contexts that offer negative moral examples and a lack of resources and opportunity.

Even more, it fails to acknowledge the complexities of human motivation. Augustine's forensic self-awareness in *The Confessions* recognized in himself (and in all people) not a finely balanced will perfectly capable of choosing the good at all times but a swirl of unstable emotions, impulses and desires, which could sweep the will off balance at any time. At the end of the day, Pelagius' understanding of the complexities of human psychology was just too simplistic and Augustine understood the mysteries of our inner contradictions that much better.[18]

Augustine believed we cannot work profound inner change on our own – we need help. We are much more like the alcoholic going to the AA meeting who has to admit they are an addict and ask for the help of their friends and a higher power to help break the addiction, than we are respectable, capable moral agents perfectly free to choose the good. We think we are free to do what we want, but that is precisely the problem because what we want is often not what is good for us. We need grace or, perhaps in the language of the Nicene creed, we need the 'power of the Holy Spirit' to work within us and to begin to change our inner desires so that we become truly free to choose the good because we begin to want to do it, rather than doing it grudgingly or reluctantly. Christian orthodoxy tells us that such help is available and that we are not left alone with our mistakes or achievements defining us permanently.

There are, of course, many other heresies, pathways we could have examined that lead us into dangerous places. We've only had the time to look at three. But, hopefully, this has begun to show how heresy, rather than offering the enticing, sexy lure of forbidden fruit, indicates ways of thinking and being that would lead us into trouble and would dismantle so much of what we value and that makes for human flourishing. Orthodoxy is the wisdom of our ancestors that warns us at the beginning of those paths not to follow them too far.

More than this, these heresies would give us a smaller, restricted and narrowed view of both God and the world. They would give us a God who does not give us himself. They would give us a world that is not the gracious gift of this generous God but (in the case of Gnosticism) the half-baked mistake of a second-rate divinity.

If it is true that this is a world that is the creation of a God who is Father, Son and Holy Spirit, as the creeds tell us, then it makes all the sense in the world to learn to live within the bounds of the world as it is on this island of grace. We end by returning to the wise words of Jane Williams: 'to choose to live otherwise than in this world of gift and response is to choose to live in empty fantasy.'[19]

8

The household of faith

Heresy is a real danger. There are pathways that lead dangerously close to the edge of the cliff. Yet, despite this, the island is large. There is much to discover and, even within the Christian Church, there is ample scope for exploration, discussion and creative thinking.

Churches come in different sizes, shapes and situations. They also look and feel very different. Across the world, the Church meets in grand cathedrals, under trees, in tin shacks and in ordinary homes. In my role as a bishop in the Church of England, I can worship in one church in the morning with written liturgy, elaborate robes, formal gestures, incense, candles and statues of the Virgin Mary, and another in the evening with a contemporary worship band, extempore praise, singing in tongues and prayer ministry, led by ministers in jeans and jackets. Yet they are both part of the same Church.

Down the years, the Church has developed a dizzyingly wide variety of styles or expressions, some explained by differences of cultural context, some by theological differences of conviction, some by personal preference. Some of those divisions are the result of actual splits or schisms in the past, some are held within the bounds of one particular denomination. Whatever else it is, Christianity is not monochrome.

Rooms and hallways

In the preface to *Mere Christianity*, C. S. Lewis wrote about how, in the book, he had deliberately tried to steer clear of disputed points in theology and the differences between Christian denominations.

This was because he was writing mainly for a non-believing audience and wanted to portray a more generalized picture of Christianity, one that most Christians of whatever church could recognize. He described the kind of Christianity he was writing about in relation to the different expressions of the Church like this:

> It is more like a hall out of which doors open into several rooms. If I can bring anyone into that hall, I shall have done what I attempted. But it is in the rooms, not the hall, that there are fires and chairs and meals. The hall is a place to wait in, a place from which to try the various doors, not a place to live in. For that purpose, the worst of the rooms (whichever that may be), is, I think, preferable.[1]

It's a good description of the kind of Christianity we have been exploring in this book: the 'generous orthodoxy' of the creeds.

When you think of it, the Nicene Creed is a remarkable document. It is the one creed that is accepted by just about every Christian church across the planet – Eastern Orthodox, Roman Catholic and the various types of Protestant churches – which together comprise around 2.4 billion people, around 30 per cent of the world's population. Yet the Nicene Creed doesn't tell you much about how to run your church. It doesn't say anything about forms of worship, what music to use or some of the more precise details of theological debate. It doesn't even mention such crucial things as the Eucharist, church government or how to appoint the church's leaders.

It describes, in C. S. Lewis's terms, the hallway, but as he suggests, the hallway is not a place to live. You have to find a room off the hallway and learn to live and become content in it. His point is that Christianity is lived and exercised in particular contexts, in specific social and historical circumstances and that each of us needs a tradition within the tradition, a place within the broader Christian family in which we feel at home.

This is perhaps one of the difficulties of Brian McLaren's book, *A Generous Orthodoxy*. Coming from a fairly conservative American

Evangelical background, the book recounts McLaren's fascinating journey of discovery that there is more to the Christian Church than the particular expression of it he grew up with. Reading it feels a little like watching a child in a sweet shop discovering there are all kinds of goodies on offer besides the gumdrops that he or she thought were the only form of confectionery. McLaren explores many different rooms off the hallway (Catholic, Charismatic, Methodist, green, mystical etc.), without ending up in any of them. Because he doesn't really give an account of, or show any great interest in, the basic 'orthodoxy' of the title, he gives the impression of ending up in a rather traditionless Christianity, trying to live in all the rooms at once or perhaps even back in the hallway. It also gives him no criteria with which to discern which developments in Christian history and theology are authentic and which are not. It may also explain why some parts of the 'Emerging Church' movement have found it difficult to establish a longer-term presence and identity because of the failure to recognize that we each need a home somewhere within the many rooms of our Father's house.[2]

Other movements in this space come across the same issue. In the 1990s and 2000s, a movement known as 'Deep Church' gained some ground in the UK, led by Andrew Walker among others.[3] It took this phrase from a 1952 letter to *The Times* from C. S. Lewis himself and explored a broader form of Christianity that brought together the Charismatic, Catholic, Evangelical and Orthodox traditions to discern a deeper structure of Christian faith that they held in common and to unite against the common enemy of a post-Christian modernity. This had the advantage of a richer engagement with the creeds and the great theological tradition of the Church, and avoided the nomadic rootlessness of McLaren's vision. As Luke Bretherton puts it in recommending a vision of 'Deep Church' instead of 'Emerging Church', 'in proposing this I am proposing nothing new, simply that we do an old thing well.'[4]

The same is true of generous orthodoxy. It can never become a particular type of Christianity, a new room in the house, and can never be about the formation of a new set of churches, as many renewal movements over the years have ended up doing.

Of course, new churches and denominations have emerged over time. The 'one holy catholic and apostolic Church' mentioned in the creed is an object of faith, not of sight. You can view this development positively, in that it shows Christianity's ability to adapt to different times and cultures, a picture of the multi-faceted and diverse Christian Church. Or you can see it negatively, as a sign of Christians falling out with each other and an inability to hold the unity of the Spirit in the bond of peace. Either way, the reality is that we are born into or find faith in different expressions of Christian faith on this side of the final resurrection of the dead, and we have no choice but to live in one or other of those rooms as they exist within whatever local church we belong to.

Appreciating and identifying a generous orthodoxy should not lead to the formation of new denominations. It should lead to a renewed appreciation of one's own tradition and church yet at the same time, crucially, an appreciation of what other expressions of Christianity bring to the body of Christ.

Karl Barth thought that Christian theology had no choice but to be ecumenical in character and that dialogue between different Christian traditions was necessary.[5] This isn't, however, because a plurality of perspectives is valuable in itself, as if diversity is an unqualified good. It is because theology is about listening to God's Word in Christ and the Scriptures, and listening to others may enable us to hear something in the Word that we have missed. Another way to put this is that attention to the multiplicity of voices and expressions of Christian faith is important because of the eschatological and provisional nature of Christian theology. In this age, we see through a glass darkly. All of our theologies in response to God's revelation in Christ are, to that extent, provisional, and need to be constantly reformed and checked by the perspectives of others. We are back with the idea of heresy as theology done on our own. Good theology needs the whole Church.

Implicit within this idea of a generous orthodoxy, therefore, is that each Christian acknowledges, owns and values their own tradition for what it is but, in conversation with other traditions, both appreciates the strengths and weaknesses of their own tradition and what can be learned from others. So, it is perfectly fine to be an Evangelical, a Charismatic, a Catholic, a Calvinist, a Pentecostal, a Baptist and so on. What does not work is to believe that my own tradition is somehow final and there is nothing to learn from Christians who inhabit other parts of the Christian faith. We live in and value our own rooms yet we can learn a great deal by passing through the hallway to visit the rooms of others. At the end of the day, we may choose to switch rooms – people do change from Evangelicals into Catholics, from Orthodox to Anglican, or from conservative to Charismatic and vice versa – but usually, the best outcome is, having seen new things in the rooms of others, to return to one's own room, perhaps with a sense of the need for a slight rearranging of the furniture.

Learning from difference

One way of approaching the variety of forms of Christian faith is described in an approach called 'receptive ecumenism'.[6] In this initiative, the ecumenical task is not so much to find agreed forms of wording and overcome difference by establishing common statements of faith, but for each particular tradition to recognize what it can learn from others and what it can teach others as well. It has therefore been described as a corporate exercise in theological humility, which requires a secure confidence in one's own tradition yet a willingness to gain from the insights of others even when there is genuine disagreement. Here again, there is an eschatological focus, in that each of the different Christian traditions is understood to be on a pathway to a goal that all will one day share, but which no single tradition has the monopoly on describing. This is not a retreat into relativism, having to accept all traditions as equally valid with each other. It is quite possible to believe one's own tradition to be more faithful and true to the heart of Christian faith than others, while also recognizing that it still lacks the perfection of the age to come and adopting the humility that enables it to learn from the insights of others.

To show how this works, we will examine some of the main-stream traditions of the Church to describe their particularities and what they offer each other. If we take that seminal statement at the start of John's Gospel, 'the Word became flesh and lived among us' (John 1.14), these three traditions of the Church focus on three different parts of this simple yet unfathomably rich statement.

Evangelicals

The various kinds of Evangelicalism in world Christianity all derive, historically at least, from that seminal moment in October 1517 when Martin Luther protested against the abuse of indulgences, sparking what eventually became the Protestant Reformation of the sixteenth century. It is significant that the protest began with a written document, with words. Protestantism has always held at its heart a recognition that God had spoken his Word to us in Jesus Christ: it is the *Word* that has become flesh. Luther himself would describe the heart of Christian faith as the promise of God and our corresponding faith in that promise. From this essential insight comes Protestantism's focus on the Bible as being, or witnessing to, or conveying this essential Word of God spoken to the human race.

This also shows up in the Evangelical emphasis upon preaching or Bible study as a core activity of Christian worship. Different Christian traditions conduct worship with similar elements including prayers, sacraments, sermons, congregational gather-ings, singing, laying on hands, baptism and so on. Different traditions will lay an emphasis on particular elements within this list as the primary place in which they expect God to be particu-larly encountered. As a general rule, Evangelical Protestants will focus on the sermon or the reading of the Bible as the place where God makes himself most truly present. This is expressed liturgi-cally, leaving time for lengthy sermons with the rest of the worship gathering leading up to this climactic point in the service. It has sometimes even been expressed architecturally in churches where the pulpit and/or lectern is placed front and centre, sometimes even elevated in mid-air, drawing the eye of the observer and enabling each person to hear attentively the Word of God through the word of the preacher.

In the companion volume to this one, Fleming Rutledge offered a powerful statement of the richness and confidence brought to the Church by a conviction not only that Jesus is alive but that he speaks in and through both the Bible and the Church's preaching. This is a conviction rooted in a robust Christology, in particular the doctrine of the Word of God spoken in creation, incarnate in Jesus Christ. It comes with a confidence that, through the preacher who works with the Word of God in Scripture, 'God . . . is the animating agency inhabiting the written text as the preacher is led by the Holy Spirit, speaking words that effect what God intends.'[7]

Her chapter is entitled 'By the Word Worked'. It is an oblique reference to the Catholic doctrine of the *ex opere operato* action of the sacraments: that they are effective, regardless of the worth of the minister, because the grace that comes through them is the grace of Christ, not that of the celebrant. The same is claimed in this theology of the Word, that, despite the deficiencies of the preacher, the Word of God can be heard through any sermon that handles the Word of God in Scripture.[8]

Rutledge also points out that words do not just describe reality but bring it into being. If God spoke creation into being, that creative power of the Word can be echoed in the words that we speak. When a couple utter the words 'I will' to each other during a wedding, something is brought into being that did not exist when the congregation entered the building: a marriage that can last a lifetime. Every counsellor is aware that words spoken over us early in life can have a profound effect upon the way we grow and develop. A parent who called their child an idiot, a teacher who predicted a pupil would achieve nothing in life, a child verbally abused because of the colour of his or her skin – all of these can leave deep scars. 'Sticks and stones may break my bones, but words will never hurt me', must be one of the least helpful and profoundly false proverbs around. At the same time, encouragement, praise and advice in the right place has huge potential to shape us and give confidence and security. We can be misled by the torrent of vacuous words spoken and published on the internet each day to believe that all words are ephemeral. The truth is that it is usually the words that are spoken to us, about us and that we believe about ourselves that are the most profound realities in our lives, for better or worse.

The Word of God spoken to us in Christ and the Scriptures that Evangelicals prize so much is a Word of good news and joy. It is a 'message about the cross' (1 Cor. 1.18) focusing on the sacrifice of Christ 'for us and for our salvation' that brings freedom and forgiveness as we saw in Chapter 4. This also explains the Evangelical emphasis on evangelism and sharing this Word with whoever will listen. If God has spoken a Word to us that offers eternal life, a quality of life to be enjoyed now and in its fullness in the life to come, this leads not to an introspective contemplative spirituality but to an urgency to share this word with those who have not yet heard it.[9] The Reformation was a turn away from a spirituality of acquiring spiritual and moral merit with the hope of eternal salvation to a belief that the gospel of justification by faith alone offers a confidence in forgiveness and righteousness here and now, not just the hope of it in the future. As Brian Gerrish put it, for the Protestant, this turns what can be an internally focused spirituality of the growth of the soul into an active, busy faith: 'the liberation of a man from constant anxiety about the condition of his soul is what makes him available to his neighbour.'[10] Evangelical faith breathes a confidence, not an arrogance, rooted not in a person's own virtue or achievement but in God's Word of promise.

Now, of course, much of this can be questioned. Evangelical confidence in the Word of God spoken in Scripture, whatever precise doctrine of Scripture is held, can be dented and eroded by the complexities of historical criticism of the Bible. The emphasis on the Word can seem to some a rather disembodied and over-intellectualized form of faith as opposed to a more sacramental, physical or contemplative expression of it where the Word that became flesh just becomes Word all over again. Evangelical confidence can slip into arrogance and a failure to acknowledge deeper questions, and the urge to evangelize can lead to an impatience to listen to the wisdom of others. Evangelicals need to know their own weak spots as well as their strengths. Yet, in this focus upon the powerful Word of God, the impact of words upon us and therefore the centrality of God's Word of grace spoken to us in Christ, there is something to offer to the rest of the Church. How central this doctrine of the Word is to Christian faith will vary depending on whether you identify as an Evangelical or not, but there is no doubt that this is a perspective that emerges from the heart of the Nicene Creed and echoes the theology of the Word in the Gospel of John: the Jesus Christ who is 'God from God, Light from Light, true God from true God' and the Holy Spirit who 'has spoken through the prophets'.

Catholics

If the gift of Evangelicals, in their various denominational guises, to the wider Church is a rich doctrine of the Word, Catholics have different gifts to bring. In John's classic statement of the heart of the Christian miracle – that 'the Word became flesh' – if Evangelical eyes are drawn to 'the Word', Catholic eyes focus on 'flesh'. So much of Catholic doctrine and worship flows from this incarnational centre, the conviction that, in Jesus Christ, the Word truly has become *flesh*, has entered into human life and has therefore transformed the human situation once and for all. If God has revealed himself in the physical flesh of Jesus Christ, if he 'became incarnate from the Virgin Mary, and was made man', as the Nicene Creed puts it, then this leads naturally to the sacramentalism that is at the heart of Catholicism. If God was revealed to us not in the words of a sermon or even primarily in a written book but in the flesh of Jesus Christ, then that is always how we should expect God to make himself known to us.

Just as Evangelicals believe that the Word of God is not confined to the past, a historical event in time, but is transformative here and now, Catholics also believe that the Incarnation, although unique in Christ, brings with it the principle that Jesus still makes himself known to us in physical form: offered in bread and wine, in the water of baptism or in the words of absolution and blessing spoken by a priest duly ordained in line with the apostolic succession that goes back to the grace given to the first apostles at Pentecost. On this understanding, God's presence with us is not a vague feeling that may come over us during a worship song or a sermon but is objectively located in the sacraments of the new covenant. We need physical sacraments because we are physical beings. If the sermon is the primary way in which God is encountered in Evangelical worship, for Catholics it is in the consecrated elements of the Eucharist or the mass that God makes himself known to us today, and that stands at the very centre of the life of the Church.

The priest, therefore, is not just a preacher, but is the one who, when the church re-enacts the Last Supper, plays the role of Christ, as it were, calling down the Holy Spirit upon the elements of bread and wine so that they can truly become the body and blood of Christ to feed and nourish Christians with the true spiritual food that is the only true food of the soul. Just as the Word creates reality in Evangelical faith, the sacrament shapes everything in Catholic faith. Created things are capable of bearing the presence of God, which leads to an ability to look for and recognize the sacramental presence of God in creation and in other people made in the image of God, whether they are Christian or not.

Because of this centrality of the Incarnation and the related miracle of the Eucharist, the priest is necessarily set apart as the person who represents Christ and who shares in Christ's priestly ministry of standing between God and humanity, representing God to the people and the people to God, wearing different robes and dressing differently even when not in church as a kind of sacramental sign of the presence of God in a community.

Just as the Eucharist is the ongoing gift of Christ himself to us, the Incarnation itself is continued by the ongoing presence of the Church in the world so that, in a very real sense, the Church *is* the body of Christ in a way that is much more than a metaphor. The Church is more than its members, more than a gathering of individuals who happen to believe in Jesus, but the mystical body of God's own Son of which we are all members. Christians join the Church, they do not constitute it.

The one created condition of the Incarnation was the obedience of Mary, responding to God's initiative with her humble 'yes' to become the bearer of the presence of God within the world. She therefore takes a central place as an image of the Church's response to God and a unique position within the human race, as the only one whose precise DNA shaped the existence of the incarnate Son of God. The incarnational principle, that created things are capable of bearing the presence of God, also leads to the veneration (not worship) of the saints: those in whom we see something of the presence of Christ and whose physical remains may even still carry something of the miracle of God's presence.

Now, of course, much of this can be critiqued as well. An indisciplined sacramentalism can lead to a kind of natural theology that fails to acknowledge the brokenness and sin of the world. An intense focus upon the physicality of bread and wine can lead to a kind of commodification of grace that confines it to one place, and can encourage a magical, credulous fascination with the elements themselves rather than the Christ whose presence they offer. The notion that the Church is the continuation of the Incarnation can become problematic when the Church is guilty of the grave abuse of innocent people, implying that, if the Church is virtually identical with Jesus, it is Jesus who is performing the abuse. Yet this intense and undoubtedly orthodox focus on the incarnate nature of God's presence with us in Jesus Christ is the true gift of the Catholic impulse to the rest of Christendom.

Charismatics

If Evangelicals focus on 'the Word' and Catholics on 'became flesh', Pentecostal and Charismatic eyes are drawn to 'among us'. For the Charismatic strand of Christian faith, it is in the real presence of Christ, experienced through the dynamic work of the Holy Spirit among the Christian community when it gathers to worship and pray, that God makes himself known. When the Church gathers to pray, read the Scriptures or celebrate the sacraments, it can never be simply a cerebral and routine exercise. Here, instead, is the expectation that, when the Christian community gathers to worship, Christ is truly present by the Spirit and will be immediately and intimately experienced and encountered so that, when someone comes into Christian worship, they 'will fall down and worship God, exclaiming, "God is really among you"' (1 Cor. 14.25).

So, practices such as corporate sung worship where the community gathers to offer praise to God; laying on hands to ask for the Spirit's presence and transformation in a person; direct invocation of the Spirit in prayer for the wind of the Spirit to 'blow wherever it pleases' (John 3.8); and praying in tongues or expecting prophetic words (1 Cor. 12) all become the ways in which God is known as present. This is more of a corporate rather than an individual spirituality. Rather than focusing on individual practices (such as Bible reading or contemplative prayer) or a eucharistic theology dependent on the presence of an authorized and ordained priest, this is the Spirit experienced 'among us' when we gather in the presence of Christ.

In the eighteenth century, one of the greatest American theologians, Jonathan Edwards, wrote:

> If it be indeed so . . . that grace in the soul is so the effect of God's power, that it is fitly compared to those effects which are farthest from being owing to any strength in the subject, such as a generation, or a being begotten and resurrection, or a being raised from the dead, and creation, or a being brought out of nothing into being . . . then what account can be given of it, that the Almighty, in so great a work of His power, should so carefully hide his power that the subjects of it should be able to discern nothing of it?[11]

His point is that, if God's work of creation and resurrection is so powerful that their evidence would be plain to all, then would it not be strange that the work of God in the soul of a person should be imperceptible? If the Holy Spirit really is God at work, as Basil the Great, Gregory of Nyssa and so many others asserted, then surely something might be *felt* from time to time? Of course, this is not just confined to the modern-day Pentecostal movement. The fourteenth-century monk St Gregory of Sinai, in writing entitled *How to Discover the Energy of the Holy Spirit*, once described the emotions experienced through the touch of the Spirit:

> There are several signs that the energy of the Holy Spirit is beginning to be active in those who genuinely aspire for this to happen . . . In some it appears as awe arising in the heart, in others as a tremulous sense of jubilation, in others as joy, in others as joy mingled with awe, or as trembling mingled with joy and sometimes it manifests itself as tears and awe.[12]

The Holy Spirit brings about faith, which is not irrational but transcends rationality, so it is not surprising if ordinary human language cannot cope with the foretaste of the new creation that the Spirit enables us to experience. As Jean-Jacques Suurmond puts it, the gift of tongues, the ability to pray in words and sounds that are not a human language but are still somehow regular and rhythmic even if not immediately intelligible,[13] 'helps to break through the excessive control of the analytical intellect and to make us open to an encounter with God in the deeper levels of our being.'[14] Tongues, prophecy and being overwhelmed with a sense of the presence of God, have the power to break down our defences in ways that quieter or more rational spiritualities sometimes don't. The Roman Catholic Charismatic theologian Simon Tugwell put it like this:

> You cannot pray in tongues unless you are prepared to make a fool of yourself, and let something happen to you, over which your mind has none of its usual control. You cannot engineer tongues, any more than you could engineer the kind of weeping that Isaac or Symeon was talking about, or St Teresa's prayer of quiet.[15]

In what is sometimes an over-rationalized Church, Pentecostalism has been a radical, grassroots movement, beginning with a stirring of the Spirit among a mainly poor, black community in Asuza Street in California in the early twentieth century, and it continues today in largely poor and non-white communities across the world. In an over-naturalistic world, which often shuts out the transcendent altogether, and a Church that is sometimes happy to acquiesce in that, in all but name, Pentecostal and Charismatic spirituality offers what James K. A. Smith called an 'enchanted naturalism', where miracles or surprises of the Spirit are expected, prayed for and anticipated. If the Spirit is present in all creation, then miracles are just intensified, 'speeded-up' forms of this presence in a created order that is, by its very nature as a creation of God, primed for the Spirit's action.[16]

Now, as with all other traditions, there are questions to be asked. Sometimes, the expectation of the experienced presence of the Spirit can become just as formulaic as any other kind of worship and become a manipulative, over-hyped demand for experience for its own sake. Pentecostalism has sometimes become wrapped up with a form of prosperity teaching in many countries around the world that seems a long way from the life and suffering of Jesus. At times, Charismatic and Pentecostal faith drifts into over-inflated claims of miracles beyond that which can be verified. Charismatics can become so fixated on the Spirit that they forget that the Spirit's work is to bring us to the Father through the Son, or that the Spirit does not dispense with things like the Bible, sermons or sacraments but brings them to life and makes them penetrate our souls. Yet this emphasis on the dynamic presence of the Spirit, the expectation that it is possible to have a dynamic and transformational encounter with the risen Christ today, is perhaps the great gift of the Pentecostal impulse to the Church.

We have only had space to explore three of the rooms. There are, of course, many more – Baptist, Methodist, Orthodox, contemplative, mystical and so on – though some of these can perhaps be seen as sub-divisions of these three larger rooms in the house.

To repeat, the point of this chapter is not to advocate the leaving of one's own room to live in the hallway of a 'generous orthodoxy'. It is to promote a sense of generosity towards each other across the traditions of the Church and a willingness to suspend judgement. It is to live in one's own room – Evangelical, Charismatic, Catholic, Orthodox, Baptist or whatever – yet to visit the hallway often, to wander into other rooms from time to time, and to learn from others to shape our own rooms a bit better.[17] At St Mellitus College, we have seen, on numerous occasions, students and teachers finding themselves moved and humbled by encountering a tradition they had hitherto dismissed.

Maybe in time, this practise of a generous orthodoxy – visiting each other's rooms and learning from and appreciating the good things we find there – will mean that our own different rooms within the household of faith gradually become a little more like each other. The differences might end up more about social and geographical context rather than substantial disagreement so that, in time, 'all of us come to the unity of the faith and of the knowledge of the Son of God, to maturity, to the measure of the full stature of Christ' (Eph. 4.13).

9

The bonds and boundaries of unity

The God described in the Nicene Creed is no idle God. He is busy with the work of creation, which includes the creation of time, but even 'before' time, there is movement at the heart of this God. We have already seen how, before the beginning of time, the Son is begotten of the Father and the Holy Spirit proceeds from the Father (and perhaps the Son, as the Western churches have it).[1] There is this eternal, centrifugal energy in the life of God that is as far removed from the Aristotelian 'unmoved mover' as we could imagine. This God is constantly going out from himself so that the acts of creation, Incarnation and the coming of the Spirit are the echoes in time of the eternal nature of this God who is more full of life and dynamism than we could ever imagine.

If there is this movement within the very heart of God that is then expressed in the historical acts of creation – the calling of Israel, the Incarnation, the Passion and resurrection of Christ and Pentecost – then another way to put this is that we are dealing with a God who is, in his very nature, grace and generosity. This is a God who is constantly giving. The persons of the Trinity do not exist as autonomous separate individuals but only exist in their relations to one another, relations of constant giving and receiving. Yet this divine giving is also expressed in history, offering us (in the words of Nicaea) his Word in Christ and through the prophets, the gift of the Spirit, the forgiveness of sins, and the life of the world to come. This is a feature of God that the greatest theologians of the Christian Church such as Athanasius,

Augustine, Aquinas, Luther and others all recognized: that the notions of grace, Gift and generosity go to the very heart of who this God is.

If this is true and we live in a world created by a God of grace and generosity, then to live in line with Christian orthodoxy will mean not just to remain loyal to this inheritance of faith with a dogged and grim determination but to hold this orthodoxy with the same kind of grace and generosity that we see in the God that it describes. A generous Christian orthodoxy is an invitation to live as if the world we live in really was created by this good, generous, gracious God who is Father, Son and Holy Spirit.

Yet this raises its own particular issues. What are the bounds of Christian unity? Where do the limits lie on agreement in Christian belief? And what are the particular bonds that hold the Church together? This chapter will explore this vital issue of the nature of Christian unity.[2]

The bonds of unity

We have turned frequently to St Irenaeus, as he is one of the first to consider the questions we have been pondering and the architect of much of what Christians believe about tradition, Church and unity. Combatting the Gnostics involved identifying the boundary lines between teaching that was true to the embryonic identity and character of the Christian Church and ideas that would lead it in a radically different and perilous direction, one that would betray its identity and soul. In the course of his *Adversos Haereses*, he is concerned with two things: the integrity and unity of the Church. He wants to delineate what the Church believes as opposed to the Gnostics and to clarify the difference between them, yet also identify what holds the Church together as a whole. To do this, he identifies a number of factors that have become definitive as the bonds that hold the Church together.

First, there are the Scriptures. At the time of Irenaeus, there was, of course, no agreed canon of the New Testament, however, he repeatedly returns to the text of both the Old Testament and the emerging New Testament Scriptures as the basis for his argument.[3] He identifies the four canonical Gospels as the basis of our knowledge of Christ[4] yet recognizes that there are not four different Gospels but one 'fourfold gospel'.[5] He mounts an argument that Luke wrote the book of Acts, that Luke's doctrine is in full agreement with the teaching of St Paul and argues for the clarity of Paul's teaching,[6] making the case that, although varied, the Scriptures speak with a common voice.

At the same time, he is aware that his Gnostic opponents use these same texts to argue their own point of view and therefore he has to suggest criteria that enable Scripture to be read in line with what he considers the true apostolic tradition as handed on from the beginning. So, at several points, he outlines an early version of the creed, a summary of Christian belief that derives from the earlier *regula fidei*, an outline whose contours are repeated throughout his book and that is not too dissimilar to the later Apostles' Creed.[7]

How then, is that faith to be preserved, conserved and developed in the various contexts in which the Church finds itself? Irenaeus then considers the need for particular people who bear the responsibility for this task: bishops. He introduces the idea of the apostolic succession, a transparent line of authority from the original followers of Jesus to the bishops who inherited many of their functions within the Church. He does this precisely because of the Gnostic charge that there were secret teachings that ordinary people do not know, that were handed on privately from the original apostles and that made their way to the Gnostic teachers. Irenaeus claims that, if he had time, he could name the line of bishops in different parts of the Christian world who would surely have known any hidden teachings that came from the original apostles: 'If . . . the apostles had known secret mysteries that they would have taught secretly to the "perfect", unknown to the others, they would certainly have transmitted them especially to those to whom they entrusted the churches.'[8] Bishops (or perhaps their equivalent in non-episcopal churches) therefore have the mandate and responsibility to continue this process of preservation and handing on of the apostolic tradition intact while respecting the different languages and cultures in which the Church finds itself.

Bishops, or their equivalent, thus represent the personal aspect of the Church's unity. As those charged with the responsibility to keep the Church true to its identity, they preserve the sense that the bonds that hold the Church together are not just institutional or doctrinal but personal. The unity of the Church is held not just in a constitution or a formula but by the intimate bonds between the bishop and his or her people.[9]

We might add one more bond of unity. How are we to recognize other members of this Church? The Nicene Creed, perhaps surprisingly, mentions only one sacrament in relation to what it says about the Church: baptism:

> We believe in one holy catholic and apostolic Church.
> We acknowledge one baptism for the forgiveness of sins.

The emphasis in both clauses is on 'one'. Despite the many different denominations and expressions of Church across the world, in the eyes of God there is only one Church and only one baptism for the forgiveness of sins that is the mode of entry into that Church. Irenaeus, as well as the later fathers of Nicaea, was aware that not everyone was a member of this Church. Even in the days of Christendom, when membership of the Church was the default position for most people in Europe, there was still the need for some identification marker, a point of initiation into this Church that distinguished it from physical birth. We are not born Christians. Physical birth is not the same as the new birth.

Over the years, it has been tempting to try to substitute other criteria for membership of the Church, whether signing covenants, giving membership certificates, passing tests of orthodoxy, providing evidence of a transformed life and so on. These might be perfectly valid practices and carry some importance, yet it is notoriously difficult to look into the heart of another person and discern whether their faith is genuine or their conversion real. I might have doubts as to the depth or sincerity of the faith of someone else who claims to be a Christian, and they might have the same doubts about me, but baptism gives us something objective to mark us out to each other.

The wisdom of the Church expressed in this creed is that we recognize our fellow Christians as those who have been baptized into this one Church and one faith in the name of the same Father, Son and Holy Spirit. Baptism also places the emphasis on what God does to us as opposed to our personal action of faith. To take an example from another period of the Church's history, Martin Luther knew only too well that focusing on the strength and quality of a person's own faith places Christian identity on to a rather precarious foundation. Feelings and convictions wax and wane with seasons and moods, yet baptism is something that stands in the past history of a person's life and can give something objective to rely on to name us as Christian.

This is what Luther meant when he wrote, 'we must have no doubt whatever that, once we have been baptised, we are saved.'[10] It was not that he believed in some automatic gift of salvation given in baptism, irrespective of and unrelated to faith. The emphasis here is precisely on placing faith in the God who inscribed his indelible mark upon us in our baptism like an invisible spiritual tattoo that marks out who we belong to. He goes on to say, 'unless faith is present or is conferred in baptism, baptism will profit us nothing'. As Augustine had argued earlier, baptism is like an uncashed cheque that needs faith to make it active. But it is a cheque that contains the promise of payment, nonetheless. Faith is required, but it is precisely baptism and faith in the promise of God embodied and displayed in the water of baptism that is the sign of belonging to the Church and of the forgiveness of sins.

Scriptures, creeds, bishops and baptism. All of these together make up the bonds of the Church that unite it and preserve its continued existence in time. This is *traditio* (tradition), both the content of this faith and the process by which it is handed on or handed over from one generation to the next, and Irenaeus wanted to insist that this process of *traditio* is quite plain and open, not secretive or devious. Each of these elements plays a different role in tradition – the Scriptures as the written reference point to which the Church returns again and again, the texts through which the events of God's self-revelation are described and interpreted; creeds as authoritative summaries of the Church's reading of Scripture; bishops as those who bear the responsibility to preserve, interpret and pass on this faith, responding and adapting to different times and seasons of history and culture; and baptism as the mark of those who belong to this Church and are called to follow Christ.

This notion of 'tradition' is what makes it possible to identify the Church in different contexts and historical eras. Irenaeus makes the point that the Church may be dispersed throughout the world, yet holds a common faith:

> If the languages in the world are dissimilar, the power of the tradition is one and the same. The churches founded in Germany believe and hand down no differently, nor those among the Iberians, among the Celts, in the Orient, in Egypt, or in Libya, or those established in the middle of the world. As the sun, God's creature, is one and the same in the whole world, so the light, the preaching of truth, shines everywhere and illuminates all men who wish to come to the knowledge of truth.[11]

The Church is located in particular places, speaks different languages and therefore embraces different cultural forms, yet is held together by a common belief, a common view of the world.

This is perhaps an idealized picture, especially when we bear in mind the divisions of the Church over subsequent centuries since these earlier, more innocent days. Yet it still holds out a structure combining the textual, the formulaic and the personal, which can strengthen the bonds of unity holding the Church together during times of trial and strained relationships.

The bounds of unity

If these are the bonds that hold the Church together – Scriptures, creeds, bishops and baptism – then what can we say about the boundaries of this unity? If these are what keep us on the island, what is it that stops us falling over the edge? The answer, paradoxically, is the same. The Scriptures, as read through the lens of the creeds, maintained and guarded from age to age and place to place by bishops and read, believed and lived out by the baptized, provide the bonds that hold the Church together and define the boundaries of the Church's faith.

It is, of course, perfectly possible to read the Bible and interpret it in a very different way from the creeds. Atheists read the Bible to point out its inconsistencies and reveal its flaws. Mormons, Muslims and Jehovah's Witnesses all read the Bible through different lenses, finding in it a different Christ from the one described in the Nicene Creed. They are, of course, perfectly entitled to do so, but they locate themselves outside the Christian Church by that interpretation. It is not reading the Bible that makes a person a Christian. It depends how they read that Bible and what they do with it. As we have seen, the affirmations of the creed also imply negation and so this whole concept of tradition inevitably includes and excludes at the same time.

Even though they derive from the same things, bonds and boundaries exist in some tension. At certain times of the Church's life, those tensions have become particularly acute, so it is worth looking at one of those periods to begin to discern more of how unity works within Christian faith.

Unity, schism and love

St Cyprian was baptized in 246 AD, became bishop of Carthage just two years later, and was beheaded in 258 for refusing to worship the pagan gods. He lived and died during the time of the persecution of the Church under Emperor Decius in 250 AD. That context sharpened the issues that Irenaeus had faced a century before, the issues of unity and integrity, especially when it came to the question of how to treat those who had lapsed under persecution yet who now wanted to return to the Church. On the one hand, Cyprian needed to stress the radical difference in being a Christian if he was to preserve the identity of the Church and strengthen the resolve of those tempted to renege on their faith. So, at times, he stresses the purity of the Church, for example, in his treatise *De Lapsis* (On the Fallen), rejecting a proposal to allow the lapsed back into the Church easily as a false peace, allowing tainted hands and lips to touch the pure sacrament. Absolution is possible, but only with and after a strict penance that shows the genuineness of remorse. The lapsed must henceforth live a truly and especially penitential life.

On the other hand, when writing to those wanting to take an ultra-strict line who felt there was no way back in for the lapsed and who advocated breaking away from a compromised Church that was willing to admit these sinners back under these conditions, he emphasized the unity of the Church. Reminiscent of Irenaeus' notion of the essential oneness of the Church, he writes:

> God is one and Christ is one, and his church and faith are one, and the people joined together with the glue of concord into the unbroken unity of the body. It is not possible for the unity to be rent asunder, nor the one body to be divided by the tearing apart of the structure. Whatever splits off from the parent tree is not able to live and breathe apart from it. It loses the essential nature of health.[12]

The image of the bough broken off from the tree is familiar in this debate and recalls Jesus' parable of the vine and the branches in John 15. The lesson is clear: separate from the Church and you separate from Christ because the Church is his body.

The debate over the conditions (if any) on which the lapsed should be allowed back into the Church did not go away. It reared its head again in North Africa in the fourth and early fifth centuries. Just as Cyprian had dealt with the aftermath of the Decian persecutions of the mid-third century, the Diocletian persecutions at the start of the fourth raised similar issues.

When Caecilian was elected Bishop of Carthage in 307 AD, one or two of the bishops who consecrated him were suspected of being *traditores,* those who had betrayed the faith during the persecutions. Soon after, some other bishops objected to his election and a second gathering elected Majorinus as a rival bishop. When he died in 313, Donatus was elected in his place, a man who will be forever associated with the movement named after him: Donatism. Before he lost interest in the quarrel, the emperor Constantine declared Caecilian the true Bishop of Carthage, however the Donatist party refused to accept the verdict and other attempts to resolve the issue didn't work. The Donatist church was at its height in the 390s, when the majority of the North African church was Donatist.[13] It was a divisive, angry dispute that split towns, villages and families and often turned physically violent, with Donatist gangs known as *Circumcelliones* beating up Catholic bishops (although there is evidence that the Catholics also used private militia in their cause too). Donatism eventually declined partly because of internal divisions, but also because they found as an opponent one of the early Church's greatest theologians and rhetoricians: St Augustine.

The argument between Augustine and the Donatists can be said to be an argument over the interpretation of Cyprian's ecclesiology. In his famous statement *'extra ecclesiam, nulla salus'* (outside the Church, there is no salvation), Cyprian had laid stress on two of the marks of the Church: that it is one and that it is holy. In other words, as we have seen, he stressed both the unity and the purity, or integrity, of the Church.

Of these two, the Donatists emphasized above all the purity of the Church: if there was to be a choice, at the end of the day, we must preserve the Church's integrity. Impure or unworthy ministers would compromise the purity of the Church and, therefore, the true Church must separate from the impure, thus justifying schism. When there is a choice between unity and purity, whether doctrinally or morally, we must always, at all costs, choose purity.

Augustine, however, saw it differently. It is not, as we might expect, that he does the opposite (which would be to stress unity at all costs rather than purity). Rather he recasts the issue. For Cyprian, as for Augustine (and in the Nicene Creed), even though it may exist in many forms, there is only one Church because Christ is One. Using a familiar image, Cyprian had written:

> The rays of the sun are many but its light one, and the boughs of a tree many but its trunk is one, established in a root that holds it firm . . . Thus also the church, when the light of the Lord is poured forth, though she sheds her rays of light throughout the whole world, nevertheless the light is one that is spread everywhere, but the unity is not cut off from the body. She extends her boughs into the whole world with an abundance of fruitful growth, she opens wide her streams that flow forth bountifully, nevertheless one is her head and source and this one Mother is rich with the offspring of her fertility. From her womb we are born, by her milk we are nurtured, by her spirit we are given life.[14]

The Church's unity is found in Christ, but so is her holiness. Cyprian thought that the lapsed, or even heretics who return to the Church, should not be rebaptized, and his charitable reason for this is often quoted by Augustine: 'judging no-one nor depriving any one of the right of communion even if he differ from us.'[15] Augustine likewise insisted that the purity or holiness of the Church is not something which is found in itself or those who belong to it, and therefore it cannot be tainted or lost by the sin and mistakes of its members. Instead, it derives from the holiness of Christ. The Church is holy and pure not because its members are holy and pure but because Christ is holy and pure and the Church is his body. As Augustine puts it in his letters to the Donatist leader, Petilian, 'Christ is always the origin of the Christian . . . the Christian always plants his root in Christ.'[16] Christ is the source and giver of sacramental grace, not the minister, so that an unworthy minister does not obstruct divine grace just as the sun still shines through a dirty sewer.

If the Church's unity and purity, its oneness and holiness, is found in Christ rather than in its members precisely because the Church is the body of Christ in a sense that is stronger than mere metaphor, then there is no ultimate competition between unity and purity, oneness and holiness. This is not a zero-sum game where you have to choose between them any more than you have to choose between the oneness and the holiness of Christ. They belong together. The implication of this, for Augustine, is that to break the unity of the Church by schism is also to break its purity because they belong together in Christ. For Augustine, schism is to tear apart the body of Christ:

> For in the same manner as if a limb be cut off from the body of a living man, it cannot any longer retain the spirit of life; so the man who is cut off from the body of Christ, who is righteous, can in no wise retain the spirit of righteousness.[17]

Loving or leaving?

In Augustine's homilies on 1 John, the Donatist controversy is never far from his thoughts. Taking his cue from 1 John 2.19, Augustine argues that it is those who leave the Church who are the heretics or schismatics because the Church is the body of Christ and to leave the Church is to leave Christ. For Augustine, a crucial aspect of this conflict is that the Donatists and the Catholics have the same belief in Christ, in that they are agreed and united on the core credal convictions of the faith. Augustine's complaint is not that they are heretics in their doctrine but that they have taken a dispute that falls outside the creeds – whether lapsed Christians can be readmitted to the Church – and used it as a reason to turn away from their Christian brothers and sisters.

In these sermons, Augustine has to tackle the difficult Johannine claim that 'those who have been born of God do not sin' (1 John 3.9). He argues that to sin is to deliberately act against the commandment of Christ, namely the 'new commandment' to love one another. An infallible sign of being born of God is *agape*, *caritas*, or charity:

Love alone then distinguishes between the children of God and the children of the devil. All may sign themselves with the sign of Christ's cross; all may respond Amen; all may be baptised . . . those who have charity have been born from God those who don't have it haven't been born from God.[18]

Schism is a grave sin because it is a violation of love, a turning away from Christian brothers or sisters. This is why it is so wrong: because it is a failure to love. Augustine sees love as expanding the heart, making room for the other, particularly those who share the same faith in Christ: 'Where there is charity there is no narrowness'.[19] It is this narrowness that he sees in the Donatist instinct, turning their backs on the Catholics in their insistence that the only true Church is their own, their provincial, small-minded mentality rather than the universality or catholicity of the Church. Augustine has a large and confident understanding of the Church: that it has the capacity to extend far and wide, embrace people from all nations, and speak all the languages of the world whereas the Donatists only speak two, Latin and Punic.[20]

For Augustine, the importance of unity derives from the primacy of love. It is worth recalling Augustine's Trinitarian theology at this point: that Love is the essence of God. The Holy Spirit is the love that unites the Father and the Son. Love is not just the commandment of Jesus, it is the heart of God and that is why it matters so much. Unity within the credal boundaries of the faith demands love, forbearance and stretching our capacity for patience: 'He who loves his brother tolerates everything for the sake of unity, because brotherly love exists in the unity of charity'.[21] Augustine also believes in the power of this kind of love to change enemies into friends and even to change us as we exercise it. Loving my opponents, even in the Church, has the capacity to change them and also to change me, whereas division, separation and enmity narrows everything and closes off the possibility of change: 'You should love all people, even your enemies, not because they are your brothers but so that they may become your brothers, and so that you may always be aflame with brotherly love'.[22]

Can it ever be right to leave?

The Donatist issue highlights Augustine's powerful arguments about the seriousness of schism. However, it is clear from what he writes that this refers to a dispute that does not concern orthodox doctrine, and hence he sees no reason for division:

> We ask them whether Jesus is the Christ; at once they confess that Jesus is the Christ . . . If we are in unity, why are there two altars in this city? Why are there divided houses and divided marriages? Why is there a common bed and a divided Christ?[23]

What this doesn't address is what happens when serious doctrinal division erupts over credal orthodoxy, or what are deemed 'first order issues'. Christians will differ over what is a first or second order issue, whether a topic touches on core doctrinal orthodoxy enshrined in the creeds or not. What is clear is that the mere existence of sin in the Church is no reason to divide. There always has been sin and failure in the Church and always will be. Yet what also seems clear from Augustine's biblical and theological reasoning is that schism, as an act against love, is a sin, just as it is sin when the Church forsakes its first love and drifts from the teaching of Christ and the creed.

Perhaps a lesson might be taken from the great St Athanasius. For much of his life, as he battled what he considered the great Arian mistake, it seemed the entire Church had capitulated. He was exiled for 17 of his 46 years as a bishop and – as we saw before – at one point, the Nicene Creed and its language was even banned from use. It is not surprising that he attracted the title *Athanasius contra mundum* (Athanasius against the world). Yet, while he made it clear he dissented from the teaching of a church that seemed to be becoming Arian, he never left to form a separate Athanasian or Alexandrian church. He remained, prayed and argued for as long as he was allowed to and died, in 373, before the final confirmation of Nicaea in 381. In situations of serious doctrinal dispute, some kind of structural differentiation may be necessary, but according to Augustine, schism remains a sin, even if sometimes the lesser of two evils.

Of course, there have been times when genuine spiritual and theological renewal has been ejected from parts of the Church. The Reformation may be a case in point. Augustine's notion that those who leave are the schismatics raises the question of Luther and whether the rise of Protestantism falls under this same prohibition of schism as sin. A crucial aspect of that dispute is the fact that Luther did not decide to leave the Church but was excommunicated by the Papal Bull of 1521. His desire was for reform within the Church, and it is a crucial distinguishing principle that the Reformation had to gather ground outside the boundaries of the Western Catholic Church at the time because this movement of theological and spiritual renewal was rejected by that church.

It's also worth pointing out that the Reformation was not the first major formal schism in the Church – the Monophysite controversy in the fifth century led to the separate non-Chalcedonian churches and, of course, in 1054, the Eastern and Western churches divided over the *filioque* clause (although the causes were deeper and more complex than this). The Western Catholic Church was therefore already implicated in earlier schisms, and neither it nor any other church could claim to be the one and only true Church by this time. The Reformation has to be seen as a theological and spiritual dispute badly handled, with mistakes on both sides, including Luther's inflammatory language and Leo X's precipitate eviction of Luther from the Church's fellowship. The inclusion of renewal movements such as the Franciscans and the Dominicans as distinct orders with their own charism under the papacy of Innocent III in the twelfth and thirteenth centuries is an example of potential division and spiritual renewal handled in a much more creative and positive way.

Conclusion

What do we learn from all this about the unity of the Church? Augustine's vision of orthodoxy, like that of so many of the great theologians, is a capacious one. This island is big and expansive with lots of room to play. The Church can embrace all cultures, all languages, and is held together not just by Scriptures, creeds, bishops and baptism but, ultimately, by the practice of love. That is Christian orthodoxy in practice because it echoes the nature of the God that these very Scriptures, creeds, bishops and baptism describe.

Yet this is not a vague appeal to love that says that we shouldn't worry too much about doctrine and that dogma is a hindrance to unity. Orthodoxy gives us a bigger vision of the world and heresy narrows it down. Theology matters because, as we have seen with so many of the heresies, they do not give us a God who is love but one who might as well be indifference, power, meanness or partiality. Only a God who is love can teach us to love and thus makes unity across difference possible.

This orthodoxy is capacious yet, even more than this, when it is grasped and exercised in love, it has the ability to expand our own hearts and capacity for love:

> The entire life of a good Christian is a holy desire. What you desire, however, you don't yet see. But by desiring you are made large enough, so that when there comes what you should see you may be filled.[24]

Unity is difficult. It is not for nothing that St Paul urges Christians to 'make every effort to maintain the unity of the Spirit in the bond of peace' (Eph. 4.3). Unity is built not just by theological discernment but by refusing to give up on your fellow Christians. Augustine uses the image of a purse and how, if you want to fill it with something too big for it, you stretch its cloth or leather to make it large enough. In the same way, God seeds in us holy desires, longings for the city of God that is to come, a thirst for God himself, and so 'stretches our soul through desire and makes it large enough by stretching it.'[25] Unity does not come easily to those with little capacity for love. Whatever action we take as we handle difficult issues within church life, at the very least, Augustine would ask us to search our hearts to ask whether we are acting out of pique, or self-righteousness, or out of love for our fellow Christians, however much we may disagree with them.

10

The generous community

The heart of orthodoxy is the overflowing generosity and grace of God and its goal is the formation of generous people. The context for this process of formation is spelled out in the next few lines of the creeds. After their declarations on the nature of the God Christians believe in, both the Apostles' and the Nicene creeds immediately proceed to highlight 'the holy catholic Church, the communion of saints' in the former and the 'one, holy, catholic and apostolic church' in the latter.

The Nicene Creed calls the Holy Spirit the 'giver of life'. As we receive that gift of life and live in this world graciously gifted to us by God, we need to learn how to live well together. If the generous orthodoxy of the creeds claims to give us a bigger picture of the world, a map to reality that guides the Church as it reads Scripture, helps us navigate the contours of the world we live in, and helps us to find our way to the kingdom that is to come, how might it shape our understanding of living together in this world?

According to New Testament writers, the Church is meant to be the place where God's intention for human life and the new creation becomes visible, the idea 'that through the church the wisdom of God in its rich variety might now be made known to the rulers and authorities in the heavenly places' (Eph. 3.10). This is the test of the gospel, the proof of the pudding, the place where Christian orthodoxy is fleshed out or, in Lesslie Newbigin's more theological and philosophical description, 'the only hermeneutic of the Gospel, is a congregation of men and women who believe it and live by it'.[1] This is the place where we are shaped, moulded and formed so that we share the generosity and graciousness of God in our relations with each other. It is to be a community marked by the generosity that is at the heart of orthodoxy.

So how is this new community defined in the Nicene Creed? The answer is in a classic formulation of four adjectives: it is one, it is holy, it is catholic and it is apostolic. This is the radical vision of community that the generous orthodoxy of the creeds offers us. While we cannot cover every burning issue of the day, in this chapter, I want to show how this rich description of the Church helps us find new ways to address some of the seminal issues of our day: diversity, race, wealth and purpose.

One

In the previous chapter, we looked at some of the bonds of unity, the ties that keep the Church together – the Scriptures, creeds, bishops and baptism. Yet this is not all we need to say about the unity at the heart of a generous orthodoxy. Unity is not something we achieve or even work towards. It is something the Church already possesses, but which is often neglected or fractured. Essentially, its oneness, or unity, was and is a gift of the Holy Spirit to the Church at its founding. The Christians in Ephesus were urged, by the exercise of humility, gentleness, patience and loving forbearance (because that is what it will take) to 'make every effort to maintain the unity (ἑνότητα) of the Spirit in the bond of peace' (Eph. 4.2–3).

Scriptures, creeds, bishops and baptism are not enough on their own to maintain the unity of the Church and to form generous people. There are plenty of examples of how the Bible has been (mis)used to condemn and pick holes in other Christians; bishops have abused their power; creeds and confessions have been formed and interpreted so narrowly that they exclude any but the smallest group of the pure; and even baptism has become a source of disunity as Christians fight over whether, how and to whom it should be given. As a result, we have the fracturing of the oneness of the Church over the centuries into numerous denominations and expressions, often in deep and lasting conflict with one another.

Something else or, more properly, someone else, needs to breathe through the heat of our desire otherwise, like all God's gifts, these four great bonds of unity can, in our endless capacity to misuse divine favour, end up being causes of division.

The question is: how can such a generous orthodoxy be maintained? The clue lies here in this very notion of generosity. The Spirit is the 'giver of life', and yet is also, according to a long Christian tradition stemming from John's Gospel, running through St Augustine and Thomas Aquinas among others, identified with the name of 'Gift', proceeding from the Father through the Son.

As we saw in Chapter 2, God is 'the Father Almighty', first and foremost as the Father of Jesus the Son. Yet the work of the Spirit is to invite and entice us and the whole of creation ever deeper into that intimate love between the Father and the Son. One of the emphases of the Cappadocians, in their arguments during the fourth century for the full divinity of the Spirit, was that the Spirit alone enables us to worship Jesus as the Son of the Father: 'It is impossible to worship the Son, save by the Holy Spirit; impossible to call upon the Father, save by the Spirit of adoption.'[2] And, later: 'It is impossible for you to recognise Christ the Image of the invisible God, unless the Spirit enlightens you.'[3]

Without the Spirit, Jesus appears to us as just another human teacher and dispenser of wisdom. Only the Spirit can enable us to recognize his true identity as the Son of the Father. Only the Spirit can open up for us the true magnitude of this occurrence – that in the life of this first-century Jewish rabbi, we see God face to face.

Even more than this, the Spirit unites us with Christ in the most intimate and mystical union so that we can know the love of the Father. As St Paul puts it in Romans 8 and Galatians 4, due to the gift of the Spirit, we become the adopted sons and daughters of the Father, enabled and entitled to address God as 'Abba, Father', as Jesus the Son does. Our entitlement to call God our Father does not sit alongside or separate from the Sonship of Jesus, but instead is grounded in our being united with him. Becoming grafted into the body of Christ, we can, with him and in him, cry out to God as 'our Father'. In this way, the Holy Spirit turns a distant knowledge of God into personal communion. The Spirit turns arid theology into worship.

In an article in the companion volume to this, Michael Leyden argues that the Spirit is central to a generous orthodoxy and the unity that it brings. He illustrates this with reference to the Church's debates over forms of worship.[4] The reality is that the Church often experiences worship as a cause of conflict and dispute, with different styles of worship claiming precedence, whether more formal or informal, liturgical or extempore. These conflicts, he argues, can be overcome not, primarily, by strong leadership but by a pneumatological understanding of worship. In the practice of worship, we are led into the mystery that has been revealed in Jesus Christ, which is more than gathering information or understanding an idea, but is better described as encounter. It is the Spirit who is the agent and the one who leads us into this mystery – these things are revealed through the Spirit (1 Cor. 2.10). In Christian worship, the Spirit is 'called down', whether in the epiclesis of the Eucharist so that bread and wine become 'for us' the body and blood of Christ; or in the words of a sermon, enabling them to become the very Word of God to us; or on the congregation as they worship so that songs can become a means of encounter with the presence of Christ; or the ministry of prayer, enabling healing or release from bondage.

Generosity in this context is a kind of charity. This charity is only possible when worship is understood as an act in which we are led not by our own religious instincts and powers but by the Holy Spirit, to recognize Jesus as the Son of the Father and to actual encounter with the Son of the Father through the Spirit and the God described for us in the Nicene Creed. This generosity 'requires a temporary suspension of one's own deeply held beliefs, experiences, and practices, or at least a lessening of the level of exclusivity with which one holds to them. It means avoiding anxiety-fuelled caricature and stereotype and being sympathetically predisposed to other traditions . . . with interest instead of suspicion.'[5]

If it is the Holy Spirit that is active in our worship, then this kind of generosity is the appropriate stance towards different cultural forms of worship from those we are used to. It will require this posture of interest and enquiry rather than suspicion and judgement. As Leyden puts it, 'It is to approach the global Church with the question, "what is the Holy Spirit doing amongst these sisters and brothers? And what is there of God for me to learn along with them?"'[6] In fact, to refuse such generosity is to refuse the possibility that God the Holy Spirit might be at work in these Christian people in ways that can reveal new aspects of the depths of the wisdom and grace of God than we have already been able to see. It is an act of prejudice, which literally means 'judgement before the time'. It assumes that the Spirit cannot be at work here, even though that full knowledge is not available to us this side of the final resurrection.

At the same time, this is not an uncritical generosity. The framework of credal texts such as the Nicene Creed offers us a matrix that helps us discern whether different forms of worship are life-giving and grace-filled or will lead us subtly into dangerous places, forming us in harmful ways. It helps us to ask if this form of worship holds together Father, Son and Spirit; whether it recognizes that creation is to be cared for and protected but neither abused nor worshipped; whether it gives us the big picture of reality that orthodoxy offers or narrows it to a limited vision, and so on. As we have already noted, orthodoxy is all about helping us to worship well and in a way that forms us in the character and image of God – the God of generosity and grace.

This worship in the Spirit recognizes that this is not just an intellectual pursuit but involves the whole of our being: body, mind, emotion, affections. How and where that happens is, in a sense, secondary. As we saw in the last chapter, for some, it happens in the objectivity and generosity of the sacrament. For others, it is in the moment of preaching. For others, it is in the Spirit as experienced in the gathered Christian community. All of these have in common a conviction that God acts. He is not just an idea to be played with but the objective reality who invades our lives and transforms them from within by drawing us into fellowship, this holy communion with the Father and the Son, along with all who call on the name of Jesus Christ.

This is the charismatic dimension of Christian life and theology. The word *charisma* itself means 'gift' and therefore has a particular role to play within a generous orthodoxy. Of course, the word 'charismatic' can get debased into a party label alongside any of the other party labels that we use to define ourselves. 'Charismatic', in that sense, doesn't get us very far. Instead, in view here is the charismatic dimension at the heart of all true Christian life and theology of whatever tradition, which is open to and dependent upon the life of the Holy Spirit. A generous orthodoxy keeps praying the prayer 'Come Holy Spirit' because without the Spirit our orthodoxy lies dead and generosity is just an idea.

This kind of charismatic openness, this curiosity to see where the Spirit is at work, expands our hearts and our vision, enabling us to experience and recognize the presence of God in ways that we haven't yet seen. It breeds a generosity of heart and spirit in us and allows the flower of grace to put its roots a little deeper into our hearts, to bring forth fruit in good time.

The unity in the truth that Christians possess is not the unity of like-minded people bound together by a shared liking of religious activity. It results from our being drawn by the Spirit into the love between the Father and the Son, which is the life of the Spirit. The communion we have with one another is grounded in our communion with God, which is what makes the church different from any other kind of human community. Because our communion with each other is rooted in and grows out of our communion with God, that changes the nature of our communal life. We are not at liberty to fall out and divide as we would in any other human organization. Instead, we are bound by something much stronger than our own opinions: we are bound in the unity of the Spirit in the bond of peace, something we do not have to create but must preserve and maintain (Eph. 4.3).

If Christ is not real or risen, then the Church will fall apart into the usual human divisions. However, if Christ the Son of God is alive and real, he is the magnetic force that draws Christians together despite our differences. The unity of the Church is nothing other than our common bond with Christ. That is why schism, even when it feels the lesser of two evils, is an admission of a loss of the vision of Christ and a denial of the power of the Spirit that works through him to bring unity.

This kind of unity in diversity, based on a generosity of spirit that breeds curiosity and a willingness to see where God's Spirit is at work in those who look different, is perhaps a gift that the Church might have to give to the world in very polarized times. Our societies in the West are perhaps more divided at the moment than they have been for decades, with the culture wars becoming increasingly bitter with each passing year. This posture of generosity, willingness to think the best of another; recognition that we do not possess all wisdom; curiosity to discover what we might have to learn from others rather than quickly rushing to judgement and closing down conversation; and understanding that the Spirit is the giver of all life wherever it is found – the way of the Spirit – is a radical spiritual pathway through which the world might discover better ways to manage diversity and difference than some of the destructive patterns we see around us every day.

Holy

Like the conviction of the unity of the Church, belief in the holiness of the Church is a statement of both affirmation and vocation. As we saw when looking at St Augustine's doctrine of the Church, the Church's holiness does not ultimately exist in its members, and so cannot be measured by how holy they may happen to be, but that holiness is the holiness of Christ himself. The Church is holy because Christ is holy and the Church is his body. Yet, at the same time, it is an invitation to the Church to live up to its calling, to be in history what it is in that deeper spiritual reality, to *live* in a way that is holy.

If this is right, that the holiness of the Church derives from the holiness of God in Christ, then holiness is both its ground and its goal. When we go to church – when we encounter worship, preaching, sacraments and the Christian community – we are encountering something that is more than the sum of its parts.

We are encountering more than a human gathering, like those watching their children play football in the park next door, or shopping in the supermarket down the road, but this is, in a mysterious way, the body of Christ. This is a community that has as its goal the formation of holy people, people who, as individuals and as a community, have something of the holiness of God about them.

'Holy' simply means separate, different, set apart. It means being dedicated to and focused on the true 'holy one': God Almighty, the Father of Jesus Christ. And Lord knows how the Church has failed to be different over the years and has instead mirrored the boring, narrowed, damaging possibilities of idolatrous or merely secular cultures.

Being a Christian means committing to the path of becoming holy or, in other words, becoming truly, if strangely, happy. When we chase happiness for its own sake, it always slips from our grasp. Happiness comes only as a by-product, as something that alights on us by surprise, as it were. And, as all true saints tell us, it comes when we make holiness the primary goal. The Christian path also prizes holiness before wealth or success because it knows that true wealth or success is found when we find holiness growing in our own souls and bodies.

Yet what is this odd thing, holiness? It can seem such an otherworldly and perhaps irrelevant, abstract quality. Yet, if holiness is first and foremost a quality of God and if the God of the Bible, described in the Nicene Creed, gives us this quality of generosity, holiness is perhaps closer to generosity than anything else. It is the capacity to give glory to another rather than draw attention to myself. It is the ability not to hold on to things that I love and think I can't do without because I know that God is able to provide me with everything I need and that, ultimately, God is what I need before anything else. It is the capacity to feel someone else's needs as much as my own, so that I am as keen to ensure they have enough of the things that they need to flourish in life as I am to ensure my own wellbeing. It is being able to give and keep promises, remaining faithful to a pledge that 'all that I am I give to you, and all that I have I share with you, within the love of God, Father, Son and Holy Spirit' until death parts us. Generosity, as we have seen, creates relationship: on-going patterns and rhythms of gratitude, praise, creativity and love. A community of holy people would be a community of people constantly involved in finding ways to bless each other and give to each other, sustained as much by mutual giving as by individualized hard work.

Pursuing this kind of holiness means loosening the hold of the things that would persuade me that I can't live without them. Basil the Great, one of the Cappadocian fathers, who we saw had such an influence on the final form of the Creed of Nicaea, emphasized this idea of generosity as the heart of holiness more than most: 'Resolve to treat the things in your possession as belonging to others.'[7] And, later: 'Wealth left idle is of no use to anyone, but put to use and exchanged, it becomes fruitful and beneficial for the public.'[8] Money is a spiritual issue. It is all about holiness. Wealth has the capacity to get a grip on our hearts and loosening that grip is vital for spiritual growth

This means a choice. To pursue holiness, expressed as generosity rooted in the overflowing generosity of God, means accepting limits, accepting that there are things we need to say no to, just as an athlete has to say no to the temptation to stay in bed rather than get up early to go training, or to eat the portion of dessert that will put on weight or slow down reactions.

Holiness as generosity, seeing money and wealth as means of blessing others rather than safeguarding our own future, is a radically alternative way of life in an acquisitive and money-obsessed culture. If the Church is to be a community in which this way of life can be learned, it will need to exercise this at a corporate level. This means hard choices about the use of resources.

Where the Church has the opportunity to help, it will mean, for example, using land and property to help meet the housing needs of those who have little access to affordable homes rather than just seeing such resources as there to pay a church's bills. This kind of holiness is in one way other-worldly in that, in a world where it makes sense to hold on to what you have and to prioritize profit before anything else, generosity doesn't fit. Yet, in another sense, it is the most down-to-earth thing possible, resulting in real life choices as to how we view the wealth we have, as to whether it is truly ours or God's loan to us.

Catholic

In Acts 9.31, we are given a picture of the earliest church: 'meanwhile the church throughout Judea, Galilee, and Samaria had peace and was built up. Living in the fear of the Lord and in the comfort of the Holy Spirit, it increased in numbers.' The Greek phrase translated here as 'throughout' is *kath holes* – catholic. It's the only time that term is used in the New Testament. The church in Judea was deeply Jewish, with Jerusalem at its centre. Galilee was 'Galilee of the Gentiles' – always a mixed area ethnically due to the various invasions that had left their mark in the northern kingdom over the years – and Samaria was, of course, the home of Samaritans as well as Jews. The 'catholic church' was therefore the Church of Jesus Christ as expressed in these varied cultures and ethnicities across Roman Palestine and beyond.

That word 'catholic' describes the universality of the Church. In the fourth century, Cyril of Jerusalem stated it clearly:

It is called Catholic then because it extends over all the world, from one end of the earth to the other; and because it teaches universally and completely one and all the doctrines which ought to come to men's knowledge . . . and because it brings into subjection to godliness the whole race of mankind.[9]

Catholicity means that the Church has a common core of doctrine – the belief we have been exploring through the Nicene Creed – this belief in God who is Father, Son and Holy Spirit, a God who creates, saves and perfects. Yet that belief is expressed in various geographical and cultural forms across the whole world. It also reaches across cultures to span what Cyril calls 'the whole race of mankind' or, in another translation, 'every sort of person'.

To take the Nicene Creed seriously is to say that the centre of gravity of the catholic faith is not one particular cultural expression of it, but the God revealed in Christ and through the Spirit. 'Culture' is a notoriously slippery concept, but it can be defined as the 'customs, beliefs, rules, arts, knowledge, and collective identities and memories' of a particular group. To say that the centre of catholic faith is the God of Jesus Christ is to say that the only 'culture' that can be normative in the Christian Church is not English, French, Nigerian, or Indian, but the life of Christ, expressed in the articles of the creed, the 'rules and arts' of Christian behaviour, namely 'love, joy, peace, patience, kindness, generosity, faithfulness, gentleness, and self-control', and the collective memory of the Church in history.

In a groundbreaking book and in his chapter in the companion volume to this one, Willie Jennings writes eloquently about how Christian theology was implicated and involved in the beginnings of a racialized view of the world, which has caused so much pain and damage in the modern era.[10] He traces much of this to the beginnings of colonial enterprise. When Christian nations such as Portugal, Spain and Britain began to explore the globe, establishing trade and expanding their empires, there was a deep and tragic failure of theological imagination. Instead of remembering that they were Gentiles, 'aliens from the commonwealth of Israel, and strangers to the covenants of promise, having no hope and without God in the world' (Eph. 2.12) yet graciously brought into this new covenant along with Israel, these nations tended to think of themselves as having their own special relationship with God, a form of Adoptionism[11] that imagined God's choice of these particular nations for a special vocation, ignoring the scriptural witness of God's initial choice of Israel. This led them to a hubris that led to the separation of peoples from their ancestral lands and the viewing of black lives as commodities to be subjugated, bought and sold rather than welcomed into mutual fellowship.

The covenant with Israel was unique. It wasn't something that could simply be replicated by other imagined later covenants with different nations. It was an invitation to the Jews precisely *not* to be just like the other nations (*ethnoi*) but instead to be the people (*laos*) of God, called to a different form of relating and bearing the responsibility of witness to the rest of the human race of the God who created the heavens and the earth. With the coming of Christ the Messiah, Gentiles were invited in, not to replace the covenant with Israel with their own private national agreements with God, but precisely to join this covenant: to be a distinct people of God in the body of Christ.

The invitation of the gospel of Jesus was therefore 'the scandal of choosing him and thereby choosing a new reality of kinship . . . a new form of communion with the possibility of a new kind of cultural intimacy between peoples that might yield a new cultural politic.'[12] This is what the colonial moment and movement tragically missed, yet it is at the heart of the vision of the creeds for an entirely new kind of community, which we glimpse in the book of Acts and still do today, from time to time, despite the messiness and failures of the Church as we know it – a Church that is truly 'catholic', a Church that is truly generous.[13]

What Jennings has noticed is that the invitation of the Gentiles into the covenant with Israel was the beginning of a new kind of human community. The Church was not to be like the nations, defined by racial or ethnic identity. While these were recognized, they were to be radically relativized by the prior loyalty to Jesus and being a member of his body. This was not like other social groupings that fall into naturally segregated social configurations of class, race, tribal or family belonging. Rather it was to model a new kind of relating, where different cultures were drawn towards each other in a new reality – the unity created by the Holy Spirit. Thus, the holiness of the Church emerges out of its oneness, the new form of belonging that the Spirit makes possible.

Catholicity, at least in part, refers to the Church's calling to embrace all kinds of human cultures, to critique them where necessary, yet to let them find expression within the broad spaces of the Church of God. As Cyril of Jerusalem put it, 'it brings into subjection to godliness the whole race of mankind'.[14] Although it may find national expression (such as in the Church of England, of Nigeria, of South India, of Australia, or wherever), that national expression is always a danger and a temptation, lest the cultural forms of that particular nation become normative.

For example, in the Church of *England*, we can feel that Englishness – often defined as restrained, polite, white, middle-class Englishness – takes a central place, and everyone else has to fit into that cultural form. It is why we have sometimes failed to accept and welcome the gifts of black and minority ethnic Christians, whether in the Windrush generation who came to the UK after the Second World War to help rebuild the nation, African or American Pentecostals, Asian Christians of different denominations, Eastern European Catholics and many more. To believe that Anglicanism, or any other kind of Christianity, for that matter, takes one particular fixed liturgical and social form can lead to a resistance to receiving the gifts of the worship styles and forms of spirituality that come from other parts of the world, as was bound to happen in the aftermath of empire. Anglicanism's capacity to embrace a wide range of styles of prayer and worship is an expression, not a denial, of its catholicity.

We can never see the full glory of Jesus Christ on our own. Many of us have had the experience where we see Christ through the eyes of someone else and suddenly see something we have never seen before: his forgiveness of the sinner, his anger at injustice, his compassion for the hungry, his power to heal. Only the whole Church can see the full glory of Jesus Christ. This too is an expression of catholicity. We need each other in the various human cultures in which the Church had been planted, to do justice to the glory of God seen in the face of Jesus Christ. Racism is a sin. And sin always diminishes, shrinks, empties us of life. Racism diminishes the Church because it denies us the opportunity to see the fullness of the glory of God and takes away our rightful mutual heritage. It refuses the gifts that different cultures bring to it.

St Paul's determination to see the financial gift of the Gentiles accepted by the Jewish church in Jerusalem, as well as the vision in the book of Revelation of 'the eternal gospel proclaim(ed) to those who live on the earth – to every nation, tribe, language and people'

(Rev. 14.6) is testimony to the importance of this idea that the gifts of all cultures belong in the Church of Jesus Christ. The Church is catholic because it welcomes and accepts the gifts of all those varying human cultures in which the Church has grown. And if it refuses those gifts, suggesting that it only really extends to some of those geographical territories and not others, its catholicity is in danger.

This is what is at stake for the Church in the sin of racism: not financial ruin or reputational damage but its very identity as the catholic Church. And at stake in catholicity is the Church's grounding in the God of Jesus Christ. If catholicity is the ability of the Church to receive the gifts of all cultures in which it has found root, to enable it to see the glory of God in the face of Jesus Christ more clearly, then we can begin to see why, in Christian terms, racism is such a problem. Racism prevents us from receiving the gift that others bring, which might help us to know God in Jesus Christ better. When we enthrone one particular ethnic culture as the 'norm' within the Church rather than finding its centre in Christ alone, it misses the mark. If a church in any given place is blind to the gifts of other cultures, unwilling to receive what they have to give, nobody wins. We are all impoverished. Yet, if we can receive them, we might just find our vision and enjoyment of God is enlarged and, as happened in that moment in the book of Acts, we might have peace, live in the fear of the Lord, in the comfort of the Holy Spirit, and increase in numbers.

Apostolic

The Nicene Creed's choice of the word 'apostolic' to describe the Church referred to two things. First, it referred back to the 'apostolic tradition': the corporate mind of the Church going back to the teaching of the apostles as passed on through the *regula fidei*. This is the reminder that the Church never progresses beyond that original teaching, the mind of Christ in the Church, held by those who knew Jesus in the flesh. This is the 'apostolic' church as opposed to the Gnostic, or Ebionite, or Manichaean churches that laid claim to the heritage of Jesus. It was an assertion of belief in and belonging to this particular church, the church of the apostles.

Yet it also was a claim to the apostolic function of the Church. The verb *apostellō* is, of course, the word to 'send'. Apostles were those who were not meant to stay at home, comfortable in their own spiritual status or growth, but were 'sent' out into a messy and complicated world armed with not much else than the message of a God who was revealed in a Messiah who had been executed, yet whom God had raised from the dead.

The apostolic nature of the Church therefore looks both backwards and forwards: backwards to the origins of the Church to ensure continuity and identity with the faith handed down to the saints, and forwards to the incoming of new peoples who hear and respond to the message about Jesus.[15]

The Church was never meant to exist for its own sake. Its focus was unrelentingly external – on the God who called it into being, and for the sake of the world it was called to serve. Its primary tasks were worship and witness: worship of God on behalf of the human race and the rest of creation, and witness to the God who made us and the whole world. Tom Greggs argues in his essay in *The Bond of Peace* that the Church, because it is born not of a human decision but of the Holy Spirit at Pentecost, is defined by its being turned outwards towards God and the world, and is at its best when focused not on its own survival but on its witness to the God of Jesus Christ and on serving that world.[16]

We live in a world where, time and time again, we see institutions that are focused primarily on their own survival. As issues of past abuse arise like ghosts from the grave, the instinct is to protect the institution, to encircle the wagons, to resist the change necessary to older forms of life that enabled abuse to persist. In the same way, we see institutions unable to evolve in ways that enable them to adapt to new conditions while retaining their own identity. So often, the Church is no different – our slowness to admit past abuses, our reluctance to embrace the changes needed to safeguard the vulnerable, our unwillingness to embrace change, happy with the way things are because they suit those of us who have been going to church for years and quite like it this way even though the whole thing seems profoundly unwelcoming to so many outside the Church. It suggests that we too are often more concerned with survival than anything else.

Michael Jinkins points out that 'the church faces death, like all of us. The church has always, throughout its history, almost routinely faced death . . . The church is most attractive when it pursues its own vocation unconcerned with its own survival.'[17] His point is that if the Church is primarily focused on its own survival, it cannot focus on the one thing it should focus on, which is paradoxically the one thing that will ensure its survival: the grace of God in Jesus Christ.

The apostolic nature of the Church tells us that this good news, first heard and experienced by the apostles, is not just for those of us who have also heard it and experienced it from them. Like our goods, possessions, land and property, it is not to be held on to but constantly circulated.[18]

The Church's task is to bear witness to this momentous happening, the coming of God into his world in Jesus Christ and the invitation of the Spirit to share his life in intimate communion. Witness is always contested. Not everyone believes a witness, but they simply have to tell of what they have seen and heard.

This witness takes many forms. Some is practical, such as foodbanks set up to alleviate food poverty or debt advice centres to help those struggling with money problems. Some of it is political, drawing attention to injustices in social life and using what voice the Church has to argue and agitate for change when people need to know they are noticed, regarded and cared for. Some of it is verbal, extending the invitation to know this God and to be drawn by the Spirit into communion with Christ so that they can know the love of the Father. Whatever form it takes, this is the response of the Church to the grace that has reached it. It is the form that gratitude for God's grace takes: the desire that as many people as possible are able to embrace and be embraced by that grace. As Barth says, gratitude follows grace as sure as thunder follows lightning or an echo follows a voice.[19]

Contested or not, opposed or not, contradicted or not, a church that wants to live out a generous orthodoxy will be, at its core, missional and apostolic, giving away a gospel that returns to us in joy and gratitude the more it is given away. Such a church can be a model of a new kind of institutional life. What if we lived in a world where banks, insurance firms, construction companies and governments genuinely believed that their primary purpose was to serve and enhance the wellbeing of those who depend upon them, rather than to maximize profit, to increase shareholder value, or simply to ensure survival? Generous institutions like this would have a much better chance of building societies of trust and healthy relationships than what we have at present.

There are many ways we could understand the Church's one, holy, catholic and apostolic nature, but we have begun to see here how this notion of a generous Church plays out in its internal debates over worship in a world of deep divisions, in its use of money and resources in an acquisitive and covetous world, in its approach to issues of race in a racially scarred world, and in the renewal of institutions that are obsessed with survival. This is generous orthodoxy in communal practice, tasted, seen, and touched.

Appendix: The Nicene Creed

We believe in one God, the Father, the Almighty,
maker of heaven and earth, of all that is, seen and unseen.
We believe in one Lord, Jesus Christ, the only Son of God,
eternally begotten of the Father, God from God, Light from Light,
true God from true God, begotten, not made, of one Being with
the Father;
through him all things were made.
For us and for our salvation he came down from heaven,
was incarnate from the Holy Spirit and the Virgin Mary and was
made man.
For our sake he was crucified under Pontius Pilate; he suffered
death and was buried.
On the third day he rose again in accordance with the Scriptures;
he ascended into heaven and is seated at the right hand of the
Father.
He will come again in glory to judge the living and the dead, and
his kingdom will have no end.
We believe in the Holy Spirit, the Lord, the giver of life,
who proceeds from the Father and the Son,
who with the Father and the Son is worshipped and glorified,
who has spoken through the prophets.
We believe in one holy catholic and apostolic Church.
We acknowledge one baptism for the forgiveness of sins.
We look for the resurrection of the dead, and the life of the world
to come.
Amen.[1]

Notes

Introduction

1 If you're interested, take a look at this drone footage of the island available online at: <https://www.youtube.com/watch?v=ZsOsHrR45u8>, accessed December 2021.

2 Daniel Defoe, *Robinson Crusoe* (London: Penguin, 1965), p. 87.

3 Defoe, *Robinson Crusoe*, p. 112.

4 Defoe, *Robinson Crusoe*, p. 122.

5 G. K. Chesterton *Orthodoxy* (London, Hodder & Stoughton, 1996), p. 216.

6 H. Frei, 'Response to "Narrative Theology: An Evangelical Appraisal"', in *Trinity Journal 08 (1)* (1987), p. 21.

7 Robert W. Jenson, *Canon and Creed* (Louisville, John Knox Press, 2010), p. 120.

1 The origins of orthodoxy

1 J. S. Mill, *On Liberty and Other Essays* (Oxford, Oxford University Press, 1998), pp. 39–40.

2 Frances M. Young, *The Making of the Creeds* (London, SCM Press, 1991), p. 1.

3 *The Didache*, 12.

4 Hippolytus, *On the Apostolic Tradition* (Crestwood NY, St Vladimir's Seminary Press, 2001), p. 100.

5 See Michel Dujarier, *A History of the Catechumenate: The First Six Centuries* (New York, Sadlier, 1979).

6 Hippolytus, *On the Apostolic Tradition*, pp. 112–12.

7 For a summary of the origins of the creeds in the early Church, see Jaroslav Pelikan, *Credo: Historical and Theological Guide to the Creeds and Confessions of Faith in the Christian Tradition* (New Haven, Yale University Press, 2003), pp. 365–96.

8 A useful summary and comparison of different versions of the *Regula Fidei* in these three theologians can be seen in Young, *The Making of the Creeds*, pp. 10–11.

9 Irenaeus, *Against Heresies* 10, in *The Writings of Irenaeus* (Berkeley CA, Apocryphile Press, 2007), p. 330.

10 Christopher R. Seitz, *Nicene Christianity: The Future for a New Ecumenism* (Grand Rapids MI, Brazos Press, 2001), p. 20.

11 Nicholas Lash, *Believing Three Ways in One God: A Reading of the Apostle's Creed* (London, SCM Press, 1992), p. 44.

12 Irenaeus, *The Writings of Irenaeus*, p. 331.

13 See Chapter 9 of Jenson, *Canon and Creed*.

14 For a number of examples of how the creed shapes our reading of Scripture, see Chapters 10–12 of Jenson, *Canon and Creed*.

15 Young, *The Making of the Creeds*, p. 12.

16 See 'Confessions and Confessions', in Seitz, *Nicene Christianity*, p. 119.

17 Seitz, *Nicene Christianity*, p. 122.

18 Pelikan, *Credo*, p. 217.

19 Lash, *Believing Three Ways in One God*, p. 18.

20 Seitz, *Nicene Christianity*, p. 129.

21 The word *orthopodeō* – an echo of our term 'orthopaedics' – occurs in Galatians 2.14, where Paul criticizes Peter for withdrawing from Gentile Christians in Antioch to appease those who wanted to keep Jewish ethnic purity within the new Christian communities. Paul claims that Peter was not 'acting consistently' (NRSV). 'Walking straight' might be a more literal translation of *orthopodeō*.

22 Lash, *Believing Three Ways in One God*, p. 16.

23 This is the mistake that Brian McLaren makes in his book, *A Generous Orthodoxy*. He describes 'orthodoxy' as 'straight thinking', which is why the nature or goodness of orthodoxy is never really explored in the book and gets rather short shrift as the less exciting half of the partnership between generosity and orthodoxy. See Brian McLaren, *A Generous Orthodoxy* (Grand Rapids MI, Zondervan, 2004), p. 23.

24 Nicolas Zernov, *Eastern Christendom: A Study of the Origin and*

Development of the Eastern Orthodox Church (London, Weidenfeld and Nicolson, 1963), p. 228.

25 Jean Daniélou, *From Glory to Glory: Texts from Gregory of Nyssa's Mystical Writings* (Crestwood NY, St Vladimir's Seminary Press, 2001), p. 184.

26 Daniélou, *From Glory to Glory*, p. 186.

27 See Ellen T. Charry, *By the Renewing of Your Minds: The Pastoral Function of Christian Doctrine* (New York, Oxford University Press, 1997), p. 18.

2 Creator of heaven and earth

1 See Jonathan Haidt, *The Righteous Mind: Why Good People are Divided by Politics and Religion* (London, Penguin, 2013).

2 Gilbert C. Meilaender, *The Theory and Practice of Virtue* (Notre Dame, University of Notre Dame Press, 1984), p. 72.

3 See Patrick J. Deneen, *Why Liberalism Failed* (New Haven, Yale University Press, 2018).

4 H. Rosa, 'Dynamic Stabilization, the Triple A Approach to the Good Life, and the Resonance Conception', in *Questions de Communication 31* (2017).

5 Christian Smith, *Moral, Believing Animals: Human Personhood and Culture* (Oxford, Oxford University Press, 2003), p. 46. Italics his.

6 See James K. A. Smith, *Desiring the Kingdom: Worship, Worldview and Cultural Formation* (Grand Rapids MI, Baker Academic, 2009). See also Smith's chapter in the companion volume to this book: James K. A. Smith, 'The Art of Hope: Imagining another world in a world that breaks our hearts', in Graham Tomlin and Nathan Eddy, eds, *The Bond of Peace: Exploring Generous Orthodoxy* (London, SPCK, 2021), pp. 33–47.

7 Eastern and Western Christians differ over whether to include the *filoque* clause, which concerns whether the Holy Spirit proceeds from the Father alone (East) or the Father and the Son (West). Yet, despite this important difference, they still use the creed with or without this word.

8 See, for example, Lewis Ayres, *Nicaea and its Legacy: An Approach to Fourth-Century Trinitarian Theology* (Oxford, Oxford University

Press, 2004) or Y. R. Kim, ed., *The Cambridge Companion to the Council of Nicaea* (Cambridge, Cambridge University Press, 2021).

9 See Charles Taylor, *A Secular Age* (Cambridge MA; London, Belknap, 2007).

10 The text of Genesis 1 is a little ambiguous, as reflected in some of the translations. There is, for example, the NRSV: 'In the beginning when God created the heavens and the earth, the earth was a formless void' (Gen. 1.1–2), which could imply pre-existent matter before creation. The NIV, however (echoing the KJV), has 'in the beginning God created the heavens and the earth. Now the earth was formless and empty', which seems to place God's act of creation first and the formation of matter subsequent to that. The latter is surely to be preferred.

11 See Young, *The Making of the Creeds*, pp. 25–32.

12 Basil, *Hexaemeron* (Marston Gate, Limovia, 2013), p. 15. Italics his.

13 Basil, *Hexaemeron*, p. 16.

14 Basil, *Hexaemeron*, p. 23.

15 Basil, *Hexaemeron*, p. 87.

16 Basil, *Hexaemeron*, p. 80.

17 Basil, *Hexaemeron*, p. 83.

18 Jenson, *Canon and Creed*, p. 91.

19 See, for example, Frances M. Young, *God's Presence: A Contemporary Recapitulation of Early Christianity* (Cambridge, Cambridge University Press, 2013), p. 57.

20 Alister McGrath, *Inventing the Universe: Why We Can't Stop Talking About Science, Faith and God* (London, Hodder & Stoughton, 2015), p. 34.

21 I am indebted to an unpublished paper by James Orr for some of the insights in the following paragraphs: 'The Creation Crunch: Theological and Philosophical Perspectives on Climate Change', March 2009.

3 The only Son of God

1 Karl Barth, *Dogmatics in Outline* (London, SCM Press, 1985), pp. 65–6.

2 See Ayres, *Nicaea and its Legacy*, pp. 85–6. The background and politics of the council are helpfully explored in Chapters 3, 5, and 6 of Kim, *The Cambridge Companion to the Council of Nicaea.*

3 The best recent account of the story running up to Nicaea is Rowan Williams, *Arius: Heresy and Tradition* (London, Darton, Longman and Todd, 1987). For the story after Nicaea, see Ayres, *Nicaea and its Legacy.*

4 See Joseph W. Trigg, *Origen: The Bible and Philosophy in the Third-Century Church* (London, SCM Press, 1998), p. 96 ff.

5 Williams, *Arius*, p. 235 ff.

6 Many have seen a feminine principle in the Holy Spirit in that the word *Ruach* (Spirit) in Hebrew is a feminine noun. The difficulties of gender-specific language for God have been much debated. A comment in a World Council of Churches report argues, 'We may not surrender the language of "Father" for it is the way in which Jesus addressed, and spoke of, God and how Jesus taught his disciples to address God. It is in relation to the use of Father by Christ Jesus himself that the Church came to believe in Jesus as the Son of God. The language of "Father" and "Son" links the Christian community through the ages and binds it in a communion of faith. Moreover, it is the language which expresses the personal relationships within the inner life of the Trinity, and in our own relations with God. Nevertheless, the Church must make clear that this language neither attributes biological maleness to God nor implies that what we call masculine qualities assigned only to men, are the only characteristics belonging to God.' World Council of Churches, *Confessing the One Faith: An Ecumenical Explication of the Apostolic Faith as it is Expressed in the Nicene-Constantinopolitan Creed (381)* (Geneva, WCC Publications, 1991), p. 31.

7 It is sometimes pointed out that, while 'Father' and 'Son' are inescapably relational terms, 'Spirit' is not. Yet it is always vital to remember that by 'the Spirit' we mean the Spirit of Jesus, proceeding from the Father through the Son, so the Spirit is personal in relation to the Father and Son.

8 Lash, *Believing Three Ways in One God,* p. 44.

9 For an extended development of the idea that God's 'being is identical with the act of Communion', see John D. Zizoulas, *Being as Communion: Studies in Personhood and the Church* (London, Darton, Longman and Todd, 1985), p. 44.

10 See Søren Kierkegaard, *Works of Love* (New York, Harper Perennial, 1962), p. 112 ff.

11 Williams, *Arius*, p. 105.

12 Williams, *Arius*, p. 239.

13 Barth, *Dogmatics in Outline*, p. 84.

14 Katherine Sonderegger, 'Christ's Mystery', in Tomlin and Eddy, *The Bond of Peace*, pp. 48–61.

15 George Steiner, *Real Presences* (London, Faber & Faber, 1989), p. 93.

16 Steiner *Real Presences*, p. 225.

17 Steiner *Real Presences*, p. 214.

18 See Robert W. Jenson, *Story and Promise: A Brief Theology of the Gospel About Jesus* (Philadelphia, Fortress Press, 1973). See also the outline of the argument in the final chapter of Christian Smith, *Moral, Believing Animals: Human Personhood and Culture*.

19 Jenson, *Canon and Creed*, pp. 81–2.

20 John Gray, *Heresies: Against Progress and Other Illusions* (London, Granta, 2004), p. 31.

21 James K. A. Smith, 'The art of hope: Imagining another world in a world that breaks our hearts', in Tomlin and Eddy, *The Bond of Peace*, p. 40.

22 Athanasius, *St Athanasius on the Incarnation: The Treatise de Incarnatione Verbi Dei* (London, Mowbray, 1982), p. 96.

23 Williams, *Arius*, p. 243.

24 Ayres, *Nicaea and its Legacy*, p. 300.

4 Dead and buried

1 One of the best short treatments of this subject remains Martin Hengel, *Crucifixion* (London, SCM Press, 1977).

2 Barth, *Dogmatics in Outline*, pp. 105–6.

3 *All of this Unreal Time*, directed by Aoife McArdle, Somesuch, 2021.

4 *All of this Unreal Time*, McArdle.

5 See Jürgen Moltmann, *The Crucified God* (London, SCM Press, 1974).

6 See the discussion in Chapter 2 of Simon Cuff, *Only God Will Save Us: The Nature of God and the Christian Life* (London, SCM Press, 2020), as well as the discussion in the last chapter of this book.

7 Friedrich Nietzche, *The Gay Science* (New York, Vintage, 1974), pp. 181–2.

8 Nietzche, *The Gay Science*, p. 179.

9 Terry Eagleton, *Culture and the Death of God* (New Haven, Yale University Press, 2014), p. 151.

10 John Gray, *Enlightenment's Wake: Politics and Culture at the Close of the Modern Age* (Abingdon, Routledge, 1995), p. 149.

11 J. Hughes, 'Proofs and Arguments', in Andrew Davidson, ed., *Imaginative Apologetics: Theology, Philosophy and the Catholic Tradition* (London, SCM Press, 2011), p. 10.

12 Eagleton, *Culture and the Death of God*, p. 157.

13 Perhaps the best recent treatment of the meaning(s) of the crucifixion is Fleming Rutledge, *The Crucifixion: Understanding the Death of Jesus Christ* (Grand Rapids MI, Eerdmans, 2015).

14 Barth, *Dogmatics in Outline*, p. 116.

15 Dorothy Sayers, *Letters to a Diminished Church* (Nashville TN, Thomas Nelson, 2004), p. 1.

16 Athanasius, *St Athanasius on the Incarnation*, p. 57.

17 Horace, *Odes* I. xi.

18 Gray, *Enlightenment's Wake*, p. 148.

19 Eagleton, *Culture and the Death of God*, p. 159.

5 The giver of life

1 Lionel Wickham, ed., *On God and Christ: St Gregory Nazianzus – The Five Theological Orations and Two Letters to Cledonius (Popular Patristics Series)* (Crestwood NY, St Vladimir's Seminary Press, 2002), Oration 31, p. 137.

2 Athanasius, *Letters to Serapion*, 1.28.

3 Basil, *On the Holy Spirit* (Crestwood NY, St Vladimir's Seminary Press, 1980), Chapter 19, paragraph 49, p. 77.

4 For example, in *De Trinitate*, he says that the Holy Spirit is 'that mutual charity whereby the Father and Son love one another'. John Burnaby ed., *Augustine: Later Works* (Westminster, John Knox Press, 1955), p. 157.

5 For an elaboration of the perspective outlined in this paragraph see Graham Tomlin, *The Prodigal Spirit: The Trinity, the Church, and the Future of the World* (London, Alpha International; SPTC Books, 2011).

6 Anthony Meredith, *Gregory of Nyssa* (London, Routledge, 1999), p. 42.

7 Irenaeus, *Adversos Haereses*, v. xii. iv.

8 Basil, *On the Holy Spirit* Chapter 16, paragraph 38, p. 62.

9 Basil, *On the Holy Spirit* Chapter 9, paragraphs 22–3, pp. 43–4

10 Meredith, *Gregory of Nyssa*, p. 42.

11 See a 2016 study by the Red Cross and the Co-op available onine at: <https://www.co-operative.coop/media/news-releases/lonely-life-stages-new-study-reveals-triggers-for-loneliness-epidemic-in-the-UK>, accessed December 2021.

12 Jeremy Carrette and Richard King, *Selling Spirituality: The Silent Takeover of Religion* (London, Routledge, 2005), p. 58.

13 Michael Welker, *God the Spirit* (Minneapolis, Fortress, 1994), pp. 294–5.

14 Welker, *God the Spirit*, p. 65.

15 See Amos Yong, *Renewing Christian Theology: Systematics for a Global Christianity* (Waco TX, Baylor University Press, 2014).

16 Yong, *Renewing Christian Theology*, p. 73.

17 Basil, *On the Holy Spirit*, Chapter 26, paragraph 61, p. 93.

18 For an expansion of this point in relation to generous orthodoxy, see Fleming Rutledge, 'By the World Worked: How a Speaking God Tells Us Who He Is', in Tomlin and Eddy, eds, *The Bond of Peace*, pp. 62–75.

19 Dietrich Bonhoeffer, *Letters and Papers from Prison* (London, Fontana, 1953), p. 150.

20 Basil, *On the Holy Spirit*, Chapter 16, paragraph 38, p. 64.

21 Basil, *On the Holy Spirit*, p. 97.

22 A fine exposition of the way in which the Spirit is described as

both 'Love' and 'Gift', particularly in the thought of St Augustine, is to be found in Matthew Levering, *Engaging the Doctrine of the Holy Spirit: Love and Gift in the Trinity and the Church* (Grand Rapids, Baker Academic Press, 2016).

23 See Martin Luther's last note, written on 16 February 1546 and found in the Weimar Edition of Luther's works: WA 48.242-2.

6 The anatomy of generosity

1 Chesterton, *Orthodoxy*, p. 146.
2 Sayers, *Letters to a Diminished Church*, p. 15.
3 Qu'ran, *Sura IV*.
4 For this soteriologically focused view of Arianism, see Robert C. Gregg and Dennis E. Groh, *Early Arianism: A View of Salvation* (London, SCM Press, 1981).
5 See John M. G. Barclay, *Paul and the Gift* (Grand Rapids MI, Eerdmans, 2015), and John. M. G. Barclay, *Paul and the Power of Grace* (Grand Rapids MI, Eerdmans, 2020).
6 Barclay, *Paul and the Power of Grace*, p. 57.
7 See Miroslav Volf, *Free of Charge: Giving and Forgiving in a Culture Stripped of Grace* (Grand Rapids MI, Zondervan, 2005).
8 Volf, *Free of Charge*, p. 28.
9 Both Barclay and Volf critique the austerity of Jacques Derrida's notion of 'pure gift': that it should be unrequited, without any comeback or reciprocity at all, to be a true gift. Barclay criticizes it on the grounds that this is a modern Western notion of Gift that would not have been recognized in the first century (nor in many others, for that matter), and Volf because gifts that do not create relationship lack the power to be transformative.
10 Basil, *On Social Justice* (Crestwood NY, St Vladimir's Seminary Press, 2009), p. 66.
11 Basil, *On Social Justice*, p. 44.
12 Basil, *On Social Justice*, p. 98.
13 Volf, *Free of Charge*, p. 70.
14 Michael Welker, *God the Spirit*, p. 330.
15 Luke Bretherton, 'Mundane Holiness: The Theology and Spirituality of Everyday Life', in Andrew Walker and Luke

Bretherton, eds, *Remembering Our Future: Explorations in Deep Church* (London, Paternoster Press, 2007).

7 Heresy

1 Henry Chadwick, *Augustine: A Very Short Introduction* (Oxford, Oxford University Press, 2001), p. 13.

2 G. R. Evans, *A Brief History of Heresy* (Oxford, Blackwell, 2003), p. 34.

3 Private creeds were produced, from time to time, by individual theologians to clarify their own theological positions. Arius was one of those who produced such personal statements of belief. It is significant, however, that the Catholic creeds are, by definition, not private and that these private creeds were contributions to what eventually emerged rather than definitive. See Ian Hazlett and W. H. C. Frend, *Early Christianity: Origins and Evolution to AD 600* (London, SPCK; Nashville, Abingdon Press, 1991), p. 97.

4 Jane Williams, 'Creeds: Boundaries or paths?', in Tomlin and Eddy, *The Bond of Peace,* p. 23.

5 John Stewart Mill, *On Liberty and Other Essays*, p. 39.

6 See Chapter 1 of Charles Taylor, *The Ethics of Authenticity* (Cambridge MA, Harvard University Press, 2018).

7 Mark J. Edwards, *Catholicity and Heresy in the Early Church* (Farnham, Ashgate, 2009), p. 201.

8 See Evans, *A Brief History of Heresy*, pp. 160–2.

9 See Chapter 4 of Taylor, *The Ethics of Authenticity*.

10 Seitz, *Nicene Christianity*, p. 127.

11 For a fuller contemporary treatment of Gnosticism, see A. H. B. Logan, *Gnostic Truth and Christian Heresy: A Study in the History of Gnosticism* (Edinburgh, T & T Clark, 1996).

12 Irenaeus, *Adversos Haereses* ii. iv, in *The Writings of Irenaeus*, p. 364.

13 R. Muers, 'Adoptionism', in Ben Quash and Michael Ward, *Heresies and How to Avoid Them* (London, SPCK, 2007), p. 57.

14 Augustine, *Confessions* x. xxix. 40 (Oxford, Oxford University Press, 1998), p. 202.

15 This was the 2015 Easter Message from Prime Minister David Cameron.

16 A Letter from Pelagius to Demetrias, 413, *Epist. Ad. Demetriaden 16.: Migne: Patrologia Latina* xxxiii.

17 See Michael J. Sandel, *The Tyranny of Merit: What's Become of the Common Good?* (London, Penguin, 2020).

18 For an excellent guide to Augustine's thinking on Pelagianism and, more generally, the nature of sin and evil, see G. R. Evans, *Augustine on Evil* (Cambridge, Cambridge University Press, 1982).

19 Jane Williams, 'Boundaries or paths?', in Tomlin and Eddy, *The Bond of Peace*, p. 26.

8 The household of faith

1 C. S. Lewis, *Mere Christianity* (London, Fount, 1997), p. 4.

2 There are a number of perceptive critiques of the Emerging Church movement, of which McLaren is a key figure, for example, Hannah Steele, *New Word, New Church: The Theology of the Emerging Church Movement* (London, SCM Press, 2017). See also some of the insights in Andrew Davidson and Alison Milbank, eds, *For the Parish: A Critique of Fresh Expressions* (London, SCM Press, 2010).

3 For an account of this initiative, see the helpful set of essays in Walker and Bretherton, *Remembering Our Future*.

4 Luke Bretherton, 'Beyond the Emerging Church', in Walker and Bretherton, *Remembering Our Future*, p. 52.

5 Karl Barth, *Church Dogmatics* i, ii, 823. See also Joseph L. Mangina, *Karl Barth: Theologian of Christian Witness* (Aldershot, Ashgate, 2004) p. xii.

6 See Paul D. Murray and Luca Badini Confalonieri, *Receptive Ecumenism and the Call to Catholic Learning: Exploring a Way for Contemporary Ecumenism* (Oxford, Oxford University Press, 2008).

7 Fleming Rutledge, 'By the word worked: How a speaking God tells us who he is', in Tomlin and Eddy, *The Bond of Peace*, pp. 62–75.

8 In fact, it is probably true to say that most traditions have some version of the *ex opere operato* work of God through some form of Christian worship. Catholics will believe that God infallibly works through the Eucharist, offering Christ in bread and wine, Charismatics will believe that when hands are laid upon a person to receive the Holy Spirit, the Holy Spirit infallibly comes, and

Evangelicals will believe that when the Word is preached, God speaks, is present and can be encountered.

9 See David Bebbington, *Evangelicalism in Modern Britain: A History from the 1730s to the 1980s* (London, Unwin Hyman, 1989), where 'Conversionism' and 'Activism' are identified as two of the main characteristics of evangelicalism over the years.

10 B. A. Gerrish, *The Old Protestantism and the New: Essays on the Reformation Heritage* (Edinburgh, T & T Clark, 1982), p. 89.

11 Jonathan Edwards, *The Religious Affections* (Edinburgh, Banner of Truth, 1986), p. 66 ff.

12 G. E. H. Palmer, P. Sherrard and K. Ware, eds, *The Philokalia: The Complete Text compiled by St Nikodemos of the Holy Mountain and St Makarios of Corinth* (London, Faber & Faber, 1995), vol. 4, p. 259.

13 Although, of course, there is plenty of anecdotal evidence to suggest that this does sometimes happen, as on the day of Pentecost – the gift of *xenolalia* (speaking in an existing language one did not previously know), as opposed to *glossolalia* (speaking in tongues), of which we are speaking here.

14 Jean-Jacques Suurmond, *Word and Spirit at Play: Towards a Charismatic Theology* (Grand Rapids MI, Eerdmans, 1995), p. 79.

15 Simon Tugwell, *Did You Receive the Spirit?* (London, Darton, Longman and Todd, 1972), p. 63.

16 See James K. A. Smith, *Thinking in Tongues: Pentecostal Contributions to Christian Philosophy* (Grand Rapids MI, Eerdmans, 2010).

17 If space was not an issue, it would have been good to explore the liberal strand of Christian faith, yet liberalism is perhaps in a different category from these others. It is more a cast of mind that can, and should, at its best be found in all these traditions, rather than a separate strand within orthodoxy. There are liberal Evangelicals, liberal Catholics and perhaps even liberal Charismatics, but not many pure liberals. In the same way, it is possible to think of and imagine Evangelical worship, Catholic worship, and Pentecostal/Charismatic worship, but harder to imagine purely 'liberal worship'.

9 The bonds and boundaries of unity

1 We have not had time to discuss in any great detail the famous
   filioque clause, which still divides the Eastern and Western churches.
   It is perhaps a further example of how creeds do not shut down
   thinking but generate creative debate and new possibilities within the
   broad framework of the credal structure.

2 It will also not focus on particular vexed issues in the contemporary
   church, such as the place of women in ministry or human sexuality,
   but rather look behind those to look at more fundamental principles
   of unity that might help address those issues better.

3 One scholar has counted 1,694 different references to scriptural
   proofs in the *Adversos Haereses*, most from what we now know as the
   New Testament. See Jenson, *Canon and Creed*, p. 34.

4 Irenaeus, *Adversos Haereses* iii. i. 1.

5 Irenaeus, *Adversos Haereses* iii. xi. 7–8.

6 Irenaeus, *Adversos Haereses* iii. xiii. 3, xiv. 1–2.

7 See Irenaeus, *Adversos Haereses* i. x. 1 in R. M. Grant, ed., *Irenaeus
   of Lyons (The Early Church Fathers)* (London, Routledge, 1997),
   pp. 70–1: 'one God the Father Almighty, who made heaven and
   earth and sea and all that is in them, and in one Christ Jesus, the
   Son of God, incarnate for our salvation, and in the Holy Spirit, who
   through the prophets predicted the dispensations of God, the birth
   from the Virgin, the passion, the resurrection from the dead, and the
   ascension of the beloved Jesus Christ our Lord in the flesh into the
   heavens, and his coming from the heavens in the glory of the Father
   to recapitulate all things.'

8 Irenaeus, *Adversos Haereses* iii. iii. 1, in Grant, *Irenaeus of Lyons*, p. 124.

9 For an expansion of this point, see Lincoln Harvey, 'Devotional
   Dogma and Dogmatic Worship', in Tomlin and Eddy, *The Bond of
   Peace*, pp. 137–51.

10 Martin Luther, 'On the Babylonian Captivity of the Church', in
   Martin Luther, *Luther's Works* (Philadelphia, Fortress Press, 1960),
   vol. 36, p. 59.

11 Irenaeus, *Adversos Haereses* i. x. 2.

12 Cyprian, *On the Church: Selected Treatises* (Crestwood NY, St
   Vladimir's Seminary Press, 2006), p. 178.

13 One estimate suggests that 55 per cent of the bishops (and hence probably the Christians) in North Africa were Donatist in the early fourth century. See J. Whitehouse, 'The Course of the Donatist Schism', in R. Miles, ed., *The Donatist Schism: Controversy and Contexts (Translated Texts for Historians, Contexts)* (Liverpool, Liverpool University Press, 2016), p. 17.

14 Cyprian, 'The Unity of the Catholic Church', in *On the Church*, p. 155.

15 Augustine, 'On Baptism', 10.15.

16 Augustine, *Letters to Petilian*, i. v.

17 Augustine, *Treatise Concerning the Correction of the Donatists*, ix. 42.

18 Augustine, *Homilies on the First Epistle of John* (New York, New City Press, 2008), p. 82.

19 Augustine, *Homilies on the First Epistle of John*, p. 152.

20 Augustine, *Homilies on the First Epistle of John*, p. 41.

21 Augustine, *Homilies on the First Epistle of John*, p. 34.

22 Augustine, *Homilies on the First Epistle of John*, p. 154.

23 Augustine, *Homilies on the First Epistle of John*, p. 57.

24 Augustine, *Homilies on the First Epistle of John*, p. 69.

25 Augustine, *Homilies on the First Epistle of John*, p. 69.

10 The generous community

1 Lesslie Newbigin, *The Gospel in a Pluralist Society* (London, SPCK, 1989), p. 227.

2 Basil, *On the Holy Spirit* p. 48.

3 Basil, *On the Holy Spirit*, p. 97.

4 Michael J. Leyden, 'Liturgy, generosity and the mystery of worship in the Spirit: Towards a theology of worship', in Tomlin and Eddy, *The Bond of Peace*, pp. 121–36.

5 Leyden, 'Liturgy, generosity and the mystery of worship in the spirit', in Tomlin and Eddy, *The Bond of Peace*, p. 133.

6 Leyden, 'Liturgy, generosity and the mystery of worship in the spirit', in Tomlin and Eddy, *The Bond of Peace*, p. 134.

7 Basil, *On Social Justice*, p. 61.

8 Basil, *On Social Justice*, p. 66.

9 Cyril of Jerusalem, *Catechetical Lectures*, xviii. 23.

10 See Willie James Jennings, *The Christian Imagination: Theology and the Origins of Race* (New Haven, Yale University Press, 2010), and Willie James Jennings, 'Remembering we were Gentiles', in Tomlin and Eddy, *The Bond of Peace*, pp. 151–63.

11 Jennings, *The Christian Imagination*, p. 166.

12 Jennings, *The Christian Imagination*, p. 265.

13 Interestingly, Willie Jennings identifies the lack of a 'generosity of spirit' at the heart of the failure of the colonial church to appreciate any value in native culture and practices. See Jennings, *The Christian Imagination*, p. 98.

14 Cyril, *Catechetical Lectures*, xviii. 23.

15 For a discussion of the Church's historical and eschatological existence, see Zizoulas, *Being as Communion*, p. 88.

16 See Tom Greggs, 'For God and For the World: A Generously Orthodox Church', in Tomlin and Eddy, *The Bond of Peace*, pp. 89–104.

17 Michael Jinkins, *The Church Faces Death: Ecclesiology in a Post-Modern Context* (New York; Oxford, Oxford University Press, 1999), p. 27.

18 See Hannah Steele, 'Rooted and Sent: Generous Orthodoxy as an expression of the mission of God in the world today', in Tomlin and Eddy, *The Bond of Peace*, pp. 177–90.

19 Karl Barth, *Church Dogmatics*, iv. 1. 41.

Appendix

1 The text of the Nicene Creed is taken from *Common Worship: Services and Prayers for the Church of England* (London, CHP, 2000), p. 173.

Bibliography

Anatolios, Khaled, *Retrieving Nicaea: The Development and Meaning of Trinitarian Doctrine* (Grand Rapids, Baker Academic, 2011).

Athanasius, *St Athanasius on the Incarnation: The Treatise de Incarnatione Verbi Dei* (London, Mowbray, 1982).

Augustine, *Confessions* (Oxford, Oxford University Press, 1998).

——, *Homilies on the First Epistle of John* (New York, New City Press, 2008).

Ayres, Lewis, *Nicaea and its Legacy: An Approach to Fourth-Century Trinitarian Theology* (Oxford, Oxford University Press, 2004).

Barclay, John M. G., *Paul and the Gift* (Grand Rapids MI, Eerdmans, 2015).

——, *Paul and the Power of Grace* (Grand Rapids MI, Eerdmans, 2020).

Barth, Karl, *Dogmatics in Outline* (London, SCM Press, 1985).

Basil, *Hexaemeron* (Marston Gate, Limovia, 2013).

——, *On Social Justice* (Crestwood NY, St Vladimir's Seminary Press, 2009).

——, *On the Holy Spirit* (Crestwood NY, St Vladimir's Seminary Press, 1980).

Bebbington, David, *Evangelicalism in Modern Britain: A History from the 1730s to the 1980s* (London, Unwin Hyman, 1989).

Bonhoeffer, Dietrich, *Letters and Papers from Prison* (London, Fontana, 1953).

Burnaby, John, ed., *Augustine: Later Works* (Westminster, John Knox Press, 1955).

Carrette, Jeremy and King, Richard, *Selling Spirituality: The Silent Takeover of Religion* (London, Routledge, 2005).

Chadwick, Henry, *Augustine: A Very Short Introduction* (Oxford, Oxford University Press, 2001).

——, *Early Christian Thought and the Classical Tradition: Studies in Justin, Clement, and Origen* (Oxford, Oxford University Press, 1984).

Charry, Ellen T., *By the Renewing of Your Minds: The Pastoral Function of Christian Doctrine* (New York, Oxford University Press, 1997).

Chesterton, G. K., *Orthodoxy* (London, Hodder & Stoughton, 1996).

Cuff, Simon, *Only God Will Save Us: The Nature of God and the Christian Life* (London, SCM Press, 2020).

Cyprian, *On the Church: Selected Treatises* (Crestwood NY, St Vladimir's Seminary Press, 2006).

Daniélou, Jean, *From Glory to Glory: Texts from Gregory of Nyssa's Mystical Writings* (Crestwood NY, St Vladimir's Seminary Press, 2001).

Davidson, Andrew, ed., *Imaginative Apologetics: Theology, Philosophy and the Catholic Tradition* (London, SCM Press, 2011).

Davidson, Andrew and Milbank, Alison, eds, *For the Parish: A Critique of Fresh Expressions* (London, SCM Press, 2010).

Defoe, Daniel, *Robinson Crusoe* (London: Penguin, 1965).

Deneen, Patrick J., *Why Liberalism Failed* (New Haven, Yale University Press, 2018).

Dujarier, Michel, *A History of the Catechumenate: The First Six Centuries* (New York, Sadlier, 1979).

Eagleton, Terry, *Culture and the Death of God* (New Haven, Yale University Press, 2014).

Edwards, Jonathan, *The Religious Affections* (Edinburgh, Banner of Truth, 1986).

Edwards, Mark J., *Catholicity and Heresy in the Early Church* (Farnham, Ashgate, 2009).

Evans, G. R., *Augustine on Evil* (Cambridge, Cambridge University Press, 1982).

——, *A Brief History of Heresy* (Oxford, Blackwell, 2003).

Frei, H., 'Response to "Narrative Theology: An Evangelical Appraisal"', in *Trinity Journal 08 (1)* (1987).

General Synod of the Church of England, *Common Worship: Services and Prayers for the Church of England* (London, CHP, 2000).

Gerrish, B. A., *The Old Protestantism and the New: Essays on the Reformation Heritage* (Edinburgh, T & T Clark, 1982).

Grant, Robert M., ed., *Irenaeus of Lyons (The Early Church Fathers)* (London, Routledge, 1997).

Gray, John, *Enlightenment's Wake: Politics and Culture at the Close of the Modern Age* (Abingdon, Routledge, 1995).

——, *Heresies: Against Progress and Other Illusions* (London, Granta, 2004).

Gregg, Robert C. and Groh, Dennis E., *Early Arianism: A View of Salvation* (London, SCM Press, 1981).

Haidt, Jonathan, *The Righteous Mind: Why Good People are Divided by Politics and Religion* (London, Penguin, 2013).

Hazlett, Ian and Frend, W. H. C., *Early Christianity: Origins and Evolution to AD 600* (London, SPCK; Nashville, Abingdon Press, 1991).

Hengel, Martin, *Crucifixion* (London, SCM Press, 1977).

Hippolytus, *On the Apostolic Tradition* (Crestwood NY, St Vladimir's Seminary Press, 2001).

Irenaeus, *The Writings of Irenaeus* (Berkeley CA, Apocryphile Press, 2007).

Jennings, Willie James, *The Christian Imagination: Theology and the Origins of Race* (New Haven, Yale University Press, 2010).

Jenson, Robert W., *Canon and Creed* (Louisville, John Knox Press, 2010).

——, *Story and Promise: A Brief Theology of the Gospel About Jesus* (Philadelphia, Fortress Press, 1973).

Jinkins, Michael, *The Church Faces Death: Ecclesiology in a Post-Modern Context* (New York; Oxford, Oxford University Press, 1999).

Kierkegaard, Søren, *Works of Love* (New York, Harper Perennial, 1962).

Kim, Y. R., ed., *The Cambridge Companion to the Council of Nicaea* (Cambridge, Cambridge University Press, 2021).

Lash, Nicholas, *Believing Three Ways in One God: A Reading of the Apostle's Creed* (London, SCM Press, 1992).

Levering, Matthew, *Engaging the Doctrine of the Holy Spirit: Love and Gift in the Trinity and the Church* (Grand Rapids MI, Baker Academic Press, 2016).

Lewis, C. S., *Mere Christianity* (London, Fount, 1997).

Logan, A. H. B., *Gnostic Truth and Christian Heresy: A Study in the History of Gnosticism* (Edinburgh, T & T Clark, 1996).

Luther, Martin, *Luther's Works* (Philadelphia, Fortress Press, 1960).

McGrath, Alister, *Inventing the Universe: Why We Can't Stop Talking About Science, Faith and God* (London, Hodder & Stoughton, 2015).

McLaren, Brian, *A Generous Orthodoxy* (Grand Rapids MI, Zondervan, 2004).

Mangina, Joseph L., *Karl Barth: Theologian of Christian Witness* (Aldershot, Ashgate, 2004).

Meilaender, Gilbert C., *The Theory and Practice of Virtue* (Norte Dame, University of Notre Dame Press, 1984).

Meredith, Anthony, *Gregory of Nyssa* (London, Routledge, 1999).

Miles, R., ed, *The Donatist Schism: Controversy and Contexts (Translated Texts for Historians, Contexts)* (Liverpool, Liverpool University Press, 2016).

Mill, John Stewart, *On Liberty and Other Essays* (Oxford, Oxford University Press, 1998).

Moltmann, Jürgen, *The Crucified God* (London, SCM Press, 1974).

Murray, Paul D. and Badini Confalonieri, Luca, *Receptive Ecumenism and the Call to Catholic Learning: Exploring a Way for Contemporary Ecumenism* (Oxford, Oxford University Press, 2008).

Newbigin, Lesslie, *The Gospel in a Pluralist Society* (London, SPCK, 1989).

Nietzsche, Friedrich, *The Gay Science* (New York, Vintage, 1974).

Palmer, G. E. H., Sherrard, P. and Ware, K., eds, *The Philokalia: The Complete Text compiled by St Nikodemos of the Holy Mountain and St Makarios of Corinth* (London, Faber & Faber, 1995).

Pelikan, Jaroslav, *Credo: Historical and Theological Guide to the Creeds and Confessions of Faith in the Christian Tradition* (New Haven, Yale University Press, 2003).

Quash, Ben and Ward, Michael, *Heresies and How to Avoid Them* (London, SPCK, 2007).

Rosa, H., 'Dynamic Stabilization, the Triple A Approach to the Good Life, and the Resonance Conception', in *Questions de Communication* 31 (2017).

Rutledge, Fleming, *The Crucifixion: Understanding the Death of Jesus Christ* (Grand Rapids MI, Eerdmans, 2015).

Sandel, Michael J., *The Tyranny of Merit: What's Become of the Common Good?* (London, Penguin, 2020).

Sayers, Dorothy, *Letters to a Diminished Church* (Nashville TN, Thomas Nelson, 2004).

Seitz, Christopher R., *Nicene Christianity: The Future for a New Ecumenism* (Grand Rapids MI, Brazos Press, 2001).

Smith, Christian, *Moral, Believing Animals: Human Personhood and Culture* (Oxford, Oxford University Press, 2003).

Smith, James K. A., *Desiring the Kingdom: Worship, Worldview and Cultural Formation* (Grand Rapids MI, Baker Academic, 2009).

——, *Thinking in Tongues: Pentecostal Contributions to Christian Philosophy* (Grand Rapids MI, Eerdmans, 2010).

Steele, Hannah, *New Word, New Church: The Theology of the Emerging Church Movement* (London, SCM Press, 2017).

Steiner, George, *Real Presences* (London, Faber & Faber, 1989).

Suurmond, Jean-Jacques, *Word and Spirit at Play: Towards a Charismatic Theology* (Grand Rapids MI, Eerdmans, 1995).

Taylor, Charles, *The Ethics of Authenticity* (Cambridge MA, Harvard University Press, 2018).

——, *A Secular Age* (Cambridge MA; London, Belknap, 2007).

Tomlin, Graham, *The Prodigal Spirit: The Trinity, the Church, and the Future of the World* (London, Alpha International; SPTC Books, 2011).

Tomlin, Graham and Eddy, Nathan, eds, *The Bond of Peace: Exploring Generous Orthodoxy* (London, SPCK, 2021).

Trigg, Joseph W., *Origen: The Bible and Philosophy in the Third-Century Church* (London, SCM Press, 1998).

Tugwell, Simon, *Did You Receive the Spirit?* (London, Darton, Longman and Todd, 1972).

Underhill, Evelyn, *The School of Charity: Meditations on the Christian Creed* (Wilton CT, Longman, 1991).

Volf, Miroslav, *Free of Charge: Giving and Forgiving in a Culture Stripped of Grace* (Grand Rapids MI, Zondervan, 2005).

Walker, Andrew and Bretherton, Luke, eds, *Remembering Our Future: Explorations in Deep Church* (London, Paternoster Press, 2007).

World Council of Churches, *Confessing the One Faith: An Ecumenical Explication of the Apostolic Faith as it is Expressed in the Nicene-Constantinopolitan Creed (381)* (Geneva, WCC Publications, 1991).

Welker, Michael, *God the Spirit* (Minneapolis, Fortress, 1994).

Wickham, Lionel, ed., *On God and Christ: St Gregory Nazianzus – The Five Theological Orations and Two Letters to Cledonius (Popular Patristics Series)* (Crestwood NY, St Vladimir's Seminary Press, 2002).

Williams, Rowan, *Arius: Heresy and Tradition* (London, Darton, Longman and Todd, 1987).

Yong, Amos, *Renewing Christian Theology: Systematics for a Global Christianity* (Waco TX, Baylor University Press, 2014).

Young, Frances M., *God's Presence: A Contemporary Recapitulation of Early Christianity* (Cambridge, Cambridge University Press, 2013).

——, *The Making of the Creeds* (London, SCM Press, 1991).

Zernov, Nicolas, *Eastern Christendom: A Study of the Origin and Development of the Eastern Orthodox Church* (London, Weidenfeld and Nicolson, 1963).

Zizoulas, John D., *Being as Communion: Studies in Personhood and the Church* (London, Darton, Longman and Todd, 1985).